TWO SURVIVED

The jolly-boat at its point of landing on Eleuthera Island.
Arthur K. Blood

TWO SURVIVED

The Timeless WWII Epic of Seventy Days
at Sea in an Open Boat

Guy Pearce Jones

With an Introduction by
William McFee

The Lyons Press
Guilford, Connecticut
An imprint of The Globe Pequot Press

The Lyons Press is an imprint of The Globe Pequot Press.

Printed in the United States of America

Text design by Kim Burdick

10 9 8 7 6 5 4 3 2 1

ISBN 978-1-59921-430-6

The Library of Congress has previously cataloged an earlier edition as follows:

Jones, Guy Pearce.
    Two survived; the story of Tapscott and Widdicombe, who were torpedoed
        in mid-Atlantic and survived seventy days in an open boat, by Guy Pearce
        Jones, with an introduction by William McFee xvii, 192 p. illus. 20 cm.
    ISBN 1-58574-420-4 (pb)
    I. Widdicombe, Roy. II. Tapscott, Roger.
        III. Anglo-Saxon (Steamship)

D772.A5j6   41014977

CONTENTS

	Illustrations	vii
	Introduction by William McFee	viii
1	Flotsam	1
2	The Making of a Sailor	10
3	Overture to Tragedy	22
4	Death Ship	27
5	Holocaust	33
6	Open Boat	45
7	Course by Compass West	54
8	Death Comes Aboard	61
9	Ordeal by Thirst	72
10	Sailor's Leave	81
11	Reprieve	91
12	The Last Lap	106
13	Hurricane Zone	115
14	Nightmare	120
15	Rescue	126
	Epilogue	134
	Appendix: Crew Aboard the *Anglo-Saxon*	136
	Index	140

ILLUSTRATIONS

The jolly-boat at its point of landing on
Eleuthera Island   Frontispiece

Wilbert Widdicombe during his convalescence   13

Robert Tapscott after his release from Nassau Hospital   14

Tapscott and Widdicombe, shaved, fed and dressed
in new clothes, on arrival in Nassau   95

Widdicombe points to notches in gunwale of
the jolly-boat   96

The Duke and Duchess of Windsor visit Tapscott
and Widdicombe at Nassau Hospital   109

Tapscott and Widdicombe sail the jolly-boat in
Nassau Harbor   110

INTRODUCTION
BY WILLIAM McFEE

A YEAR ago a British tramp steamer, outward bound from Newport, in the Bristol Channel, to South American ports with a cargo of coal, was sunk by a German raider in mid-Atlantic. This ship was the *Anglo-Saxon*, with a crew of forty men.

Only two of these survived to tell the tale which is in this book.

The raider, of which more may be heard, was the *Weser*, a 9,200-ton motor cargo-liner of the North German Lloyd Company trading to South America. The *Anglo-Saxon* had left convoy and was proceeding alone on her lawful occasions. She was suddenly attacked on a dark night, August 21st, her position being lat. 26:10 N, long. 34:09 W. The nearest land was to the eastward a thousand miles or so, to the Canaries or Cape Verde Islands. Westward the West Indian islands were 2,800 miles west-southwest. The *Weser's* first onslaught destroyed the *Anglo-Saxon's* gun and wounded her gunner, an ex-Royal Marine. Machine-guns poured a hail of bullets into the bridge structure and Captain Flynn was riddled as he dropped the ship's papers over side in the weighted bag.

He need have had no fear that anything on his ship would fall into enemy hands. The *Weser's* commander, judging from the description of the attack drawn from the mate's log and the two survivors, was rattled. He attacked an ordinary tramp merchantman with such homicidal fury that it is obvious he intended to sink her and all her crew without trace. The trouble with the merchant-raider business is that a raider is bound to suspect every other merchant-ship on the ocean also of being a raider. It is kill or be killed, and the long vigils at sea, the incessant fear of being discovered by cruisers or aircraft, have a deteriorating effect upon a ship's personnel. As the life-boats of the *Anglo-Saxon* were smashed with machine-gun fire, seven men, including Mr. Denny the chief officer, got away in the jolly-boat— a skiff used to ferry members of the ship's company from ship to shore, in painting the hull, etc. In their frantic preoccupation with the destruction of the ship, the raider's crew failed to notice this little craft, which had got past the *Anglo-Saxon's* still-whirling propeller and was probably by that time out of sight.

Mr. Denny at once organized his crew. Besides himself he had Sparks, Mr. Pilcher, a young Londoner who rowed in the darkness for some time before they discovered that a shot had reduced one of his feet to a pulp of mangled flesh and bone. The gunner, Richard Penny, who was forty-two and a World War veteran, was also badly hit. Mr. Denny himself had skinned his hands coming down the rope falls when escaping. Besides these there was the third engineer, Mr. Hawkes, just out of his time and making his first voyage. He was twenty-two. The second cook, Leslie Morgan, was twenty and not too bright. There were also the two survivors, Robert Tapscott and Wilbert Widdicombe, both seamen and both Devon men, aged respectively nineteen and twenty-one.

What happened on that astonishing voyage you will read in this book. It has seldom happened that a narrative so circumstantial, so entirely stripped of all humbug and false sentiment, has come out of the depths of the sea, to inspire us with admiration for human valor and with a conviction that the young men of our time have the same courage and fortitude as their forefathers in the greatest days of Britain's maritime glory.

Your attention is particularly directed to the conduct of Mr. Denny. Like Mr. Pilcher, he was a Londoner. He began to keep a log at once and you will read the extracts from it. He found, as usual, that the life-boat, or jolly-boat, as it really was, was not properly provisioned or equipped. The breaker, holding six gallons of water, was only half full. The plug was half out of the bottom of the boat when they launched her, and they were nearly swamped in the dark before Mr. Denny discovered and remedied this. There were a few cans of mutton and condensed milk, both of which produce thirst. If it did nothing else, this log of the mate of the *Anglo-Saxon* might direct public attention to the criminal neglect of ordinary, common-sense provisioning of life-boats carried on cargo vessels. It is not too much to say that practically all recent improvements in life-boats, in equipping them, constructing them and carrying them, has been confined to passenger vessels. The British tramp goes to sea with the same old clinker-built wooden boat of Elizabethan days, with a few air-tight tanks fore and aft, with a compass in a bucket and a lamp burning colza oil which eats through the solder of the receptacle and which often does not light owing to salt in the wick. It did not light in the present case. Neither did the binnacle lamp; so the resourceful Mr. Denny said he would have to steer by the stars. He had a flashlight, which he had probably bought himself, just as the writer of this introduction bought his flashlights out of his wages when he served in tramps. Mr. Denny also had a remarkable volume, designed for spiritual support, which contained a Scripture text for every day in the year.

Things being so, it was necessary to organize the rationing strictly. They had other disappointments. There was no rain. As they made sail for the Bahamas they became parched and faint. One night they met a large steamer. Mr. Denny set off one of the flares miraculously preserved in the boat. It may have been another raider. Whoever she was, she was afraid of an ambush. She fled away and left them desolate.

The great tragedy of this log travail across the sea was the death of the mate. The radio officer, whose gangrened foot of course could have no proper care, for there was nothing suitable in the boat, died first. Mr. Pilcher, from the record and in the view of the survivors, was a very gallant young gentleman. He even apologized for the unpleasant odor of his gangrened foot. He turned his head away on the last day of his life when he was offered his ration of water, so that others might survive. It is one of the most moving episodes of the whole odyssey.

So too is that of Mr. Denny and Mr. Hawkes, the Londoner and the Geordie from Sunderland, who decided to go together, who made a simple little compact about it, and went over as arranged, and were last seen locked in each other's arms as they sank. The Third Engineer's long blond hair had turned white during the past week, and they could see it for some time, floating as the bodies drifted away. In his log Mr. Denny declared that they were depending on "God's will and British determination."

They were all young except the gunner, but Marines are tough, and if he had not been wounded Penny might have won out. As it was, young Tapscott, in his twentieth year, and Widdicombe, in his twenty-second, were left alone to face the horror.

Because at that age, and remembering what they had seen since the *Anglo-Saxon* loaded in Newport, it was horror. More than once they were on the point of quitting. In fact they went over the side together on one occasion, and together, not being able to agree about it, climbed in again, a little refreshed by their bathing activities. It rained and they became new men. Their skin had dried so utterly the perspiration forced itself out upon them in blisters, but they had fresh hope and filled the forward buoyancy tank, a thin, three-cornered affair, with rain water.

The suicide pact, of which we have only a glimpse of course, they being not too articulate, would make an excellent theme for an ironic tale; but while reading about Tapscott and Widdicombe one has small fancy for irony. They had their own private problems, which may seem queer to landsmen, but which were highly important in their relationships when left alone on the face of the waters.

Widdicombe, you see, was a "Conway boy," like John Masefield, like "Lord Jim" in Conrad's novel, and the fugitive mate in *The Secret Sharer.* That is to say, he was the sort of young fellow who later goes into the big lines and becomes commander of a crack liner. To be a "Conway boy" is like being at Eton or Winchester or, if you like, Groton. Widdicombe entered the Mersey training ship at the age of eleven.

Tapscott, on the other hand, was the third generation of seafarers in his family. Both his father and grandfather were Cardiff pilots, and Tapscott started as an apprentice at fifteen. These two boys were of antagonistic temperaments and training. Considering everything, they had to fight their dislike of each other as well as the horror of their predicament. We have to imagine ourselves there, and figure out how well we would comport ourselves. We might not assume heroic proportions. And the benevolent official who provided the Scripture calendar would probably be shocked to hear that these two young men, in a leaking boat on the ocean, actually got drunk. They had no water and all the condensed milk was gone. They emptied the pure alcohol, on which the boat-compass card was floating, into a can and divided it equally. They got gloriously tight and slept for several hours and woke to find rain coming.

This is not a critique, but an introduction. Its purpose is achieved if the reader is prepared for an astonishing tale of the sea, a tale without romantic adornments and without even an entirely happy ending, for one of the survivors went home on the *S.S. Siamese Prince* and was lost by torpedoing on the way to Britain. Now there is only one survivor of the *Anglo-Saxon.*

All these men met death with fortitude and modesty. Their lives were as precious to them as are ours to us. They were all tragically young. They were fighting the greatest battle of our times, the Battle of the Atlantic. It is not yet won. Many more young lives will be lost before it is won. This story of seven men in an open boat, if it proves nothing else, shows how little the breed of seamen has deteriorated, and how richly they deserve our prompt assistance.

May 5, 1941

TWO SURVIVED

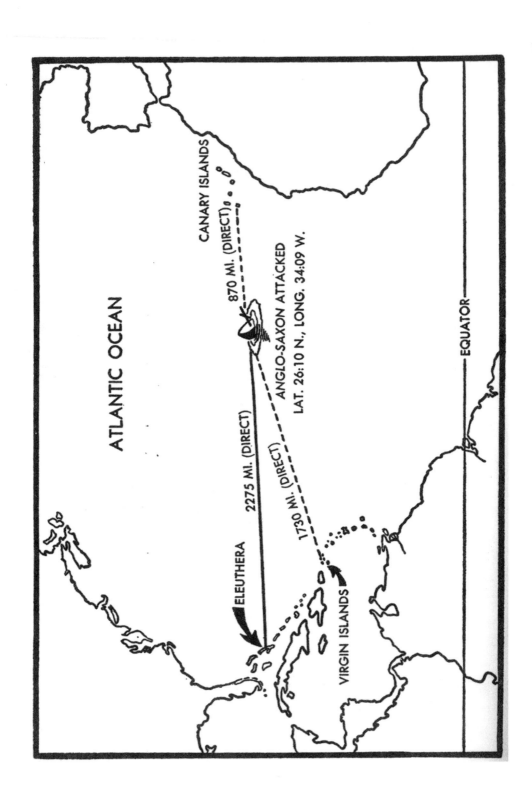

1. FLOTSAM

ON THURSDAY night, October 29, 1940, Mrs. Lewis Johnson, wife of a colored farmer of James's Cistern, a small settlement on Eleuthera, one of the Bahama Islands, dreamed a strange and compelling dream.

Dreams are important in the Bahamas; they warn of impending evil and approaching good fortune. They are valued, studied, heeded. Although, generally, the Eleutheran is an ardent church member, who has, long since, forgotten the snake gods and jungle spirits of his African ancestors, belief in the supernatural is very strong. That is why the Johnsons moved to carry out the injunction of Mrs. Johnson's dream without delay.

In her sleep Mrs. Johnson had been told—the character of her spirit adviser is not clear—to "go to the beach." There she would "find something." To the Johnsons the beach meant a lovely and lonely stretch of white sand fronting the open Atlantic at Alabaster Bay.

Shortly before daybreak they left the house, Johnson took his machete and Mrs. Johnson a bit of bread for their breakfast. They went by Eleuthera's one road, which runs ninety miles through the length of the island, like the backbone of a fish. Some distance from James's Cistern they turned east into the thick bush. Johnson went ahead cutting a path.

Although dream-inspired the Johnsons' enterprise was not altogether fanciful. Eleuthera, like a long, curved bastion, lies to the east of the small island of New Providence, on which is Nassau. It shields the smaller island from the open sea. In that latitude it is the first land in all the vast reach of the Atlantic from Africa to the New World. Strange objects wash up on it.

Combing the beaches is a recognized and often profitable pastime, particularly after a "bleak." A bleak is what the people call the northwest wind when it storms. The "rage," any violence of wind and water, is not so productive. Every year come glass balls from Portugal, sometimes a bottle from Iceland with a message in it. Once in a blue moon it is a lump of waxy, gray ambergris, redolent and valuable. Recently it has been grimmer flotsam—smashed hatch covers and broken bits of ships.

Other than this the Johnsons had seen little evidence of the war. Certainly they had no thought of it when they went in search of Mrs. Johnson's predicted good-fortune.

Over in Nassau His Royal Highness, Edward Albert Christian George Andrew Patrick David, K.G., K.T., K.P., G.C.B., G.C.S.I., G.C.M.G., G.C.K., G.C.V.O., G.B.E., I.S.O., M.C., Duke of Windsor, who gave up the throne of England to marry his Baltimore-born Duchess, was now Governor and Vice-Admiral over His Majesty's Bahama Islands.

There pretty women in the becoming coif of the Red Cross knitted and rolled bandages, held raffles and lotteries for war charities, zealously collected tinfoil and metal scrap. A Home Guard drilled and a flying club trained pilots. Some local boys had gone to the armed services. American commissions inspected naval-base sites. Now and again a business-like Dutch or British cruiser slipped in or out of port on raider patrol.

But, even in Nassau, the war was remote. People danced gaily in the Royal Victoria Gardens, sipped drinks in the Porcupine Club, swam and lunched at Emerald Beach and otherwise carried on much as usual. Air-liners brought in tourists. The homes of the rich American and winter residents were all open and occupied. Night clubs and hotels were filled. Even a group of English school children, bombed out of their home grounds and evacuated to Nassau, reveled in the warm climate and strange scenes, the terror from the skies and torpedoing on the way out forgotten.

If war in Europe had little effect upon Nassau, Eleuthera scarcely knew that it existed.

A dreamy place, Eleuthera! People with a taste for it prefer it to all the other Bahamas. Sleepy and lovely, it drowses among the relics of a busy and prosperous past. Its somnolence, the ghost-town quality of its old-world settlements and the patriarchal life of the inhabitants, fascinate nerve-worn visitors from the outside world.

Its shores are a succession of dazzling white beaches, lonely and unspoiled. Strange, brilliantly colored and infinitely varied fish throng its incredibly blue waters. Feeding jacks leap and skitter in silver flashes over the surface of its bights. Octopuses—"scuttles," the Bahamians call them—and Portuguese men-of-war, trailing their long lacy filaments, float on the heaving swell.

Round Eleuthera's barrier reefs savage barracudas flash at their prey. Groupers, one of them big enough to feed a sizable family, nose cautiously along the rocky bottoms. In the pot holes the moray, the ferocious sea eel, waves upright like a water weed until a hapless fish swims by. Like an infuriated bulldog it springs, buries it needlelike teeth in its victim and tears its food from the living flesh.

This—not war—was reality to Lewis Johnson and his wife. This and the unvarying rhythm of birth and death, sowing and reaping, the vagaries of wind and sea.

Particularly the moods of the sea, for the sea is in the Eleutheran's blood; he is never out of sight, smell or sound of it. It gives him crawfish, turtle and conch, weed to enrich scanty soil, salt to season his food. Its tides affect the movements of his daily life. Even the drinking water in his wells rises and falls with the action of the sea.

If Eleuthera has forgotten the world, the world has returned the compliment. Few Americans know its name; or, even, where it is. Yet, at one time, it was closely linked with what became the United States, and it had a hand in the founding of Harvard College.

Nearly five hundred years ago Christopher Columbus, clad in a scarlet cloak and shining armor, landed on one of the Bahamas south of Eleuthera and discovered the New World. Set a course from the region of the Azores, abandon yourself to wind and current, and, inevitably, you will fetch up on one of the Bahamas—barring, of course, hurricanes or other unusual disturbances.

Since Columbus's day the Bahamas bob up again and again in the story of America; first as the spring-board of Spanish conquest; then as the pirate capital of the Caribbean; again as the seat of the Civil War blockade runners; and, in our time, as the first and most important base of the bootleggers.

The Spanish found the islands inhabited by docile Lucayan Indians, whom they removed to a man—to die in the mines of Santo Domingo. These Indians knew Eleuthera as "Segatoo."

In 1646, a band of Puritans, wanting religious freedom and inspired by the example of the Pilgrim Fathers, left Bermuda for Segatoo. They were shipwrecked, nearly starved to death, but eventually made a settlement of sorts, complete with governor and parliament. They gave the Island its present name, from the Greek *eleutheros*, "free."

Meanwhile, one Captain William Sayle, a Puritan and former Governor of the Bermudas, organized a company of Eleutherian Adventurers in England and set out for the Island. The Adventurers quarreled with the first settlers, moved on, were shipwrecked and lived for months in the open, scrabbling through the bush and shallow water for food to keep themselves alive.

Bermuda had a Royalist uprising, and still a third contingent of Puritans set out for the new colony. Like the Adventurers, they nearly starved to death. Puritan Boston, hearing of their plight, sent them a ship with food. A year later, shortly after the founding of Harvard, the grateful Eleutherans sent the college ten tons of braziletto wood, which sold for £124, the largest donation, with the exception of the original grant and John Harvard's legacy, that the fledgling university received.

Life was not easy in Eleuthera. The colony languished. Bermuda dumped her criminals on it, particularly women. A Bermudian wife, condemned to death for unfaithfulness, was only too pleased to have her sentence commuted to banishment to Eleuthera.

Many of the original settlers went back to Bermuda. Captain Sayle, having been blown to Nassau harbor by a storm, thus discovered the shelter and moved his people there. In 1670, hoping to revive the colony, the English Crown gave it to six of the noble proprietors of South Carolina.

The new owners moved the government from Eleuthera to Nassau. They made elaborate plans but furnished little in the way of money or men. French and Spanish raided it. Piracy grew and flourished. Within easy striking distance of the plate fleet of Spain and the northern and eastern trading lanes, the Bahamian buccaneers became the scourge of the Caribbean. The government complained but the proprietors did nothing.

Governor after governor was sent out from England to deal with the situation. They were either ignored, or, worse, turned pirates themselves.

Exasperated, the Bristol merchants, the chief sufferers, so deafened the Crown with complaint that the colony was taken over in 1718. Captain Woodes Rogers, the discoverer of Alexander Selkirk, the original Robinson Crusoe, was sent to clean up. Nearly a thousand pirates surrendered. The rest fled.

Eleuthera had her share of these troubles. The event that made it what it is today, however, was the American Revolution. Loyalists from New England, New York, Virginia, North Carolina, South Carolina, Georgia and Florida flocked to the Bahamas. Their slaves came with them; six or seven thousand of them. The newcomers took up land, planted cotton and built plantation houses, the remains of which may be seen today. Eleuthera was busy and prosperous.

But, early in the eighteenth century, the cotton industry declined in England. Exhaustion of the soil, insect pests and, finally, the abolition of slavery in 1838 ended this pastoral dream. Proprietors emigrated; plantations went back to bush; manor houses to ruin. The freed slaves scratched for a living in the debris.

Many of the remaining inhabitants took to wrecking. It was seriously carried on as a business, controlled by license.

While Nassau was having its contraband, bootlegging and tourist booms, Eleuthera slumbered. Twenty years ago the main settlement, Governor's Harbor, had some prosperity from the pineapple trade. Competition from Florida and the Hawaiian Islands ended even that. Most of the leading citizens left for Nassau or the United States, Eleuthera went back to sleep. The island retains its primitive simplicity. Houses are readily put together with rubble and thatch. Subsistence crops grow easily; the sea abounds with fish. Why bother about anything else?

Lewis Johnson had been working at Hatchet Bay, which is not far from James's Cistern. He had left it only the day before Mrs. Johnson had her lucky dream. As he slashed his way through the bush toward

Alabaster Bay, he and his wife discussed his leaving, possibly with some acrimony. But the real argument developed over the dream.

Mrs. Johnson felt that when they reached the beach they should go north. It had not been *his* dream, Johnson admitted, but he, equally strong in premonition, was convinced they should go south. Mrs. Johnson was not easily persuaded. She was still pressing her point when they neared the beach.

The bush was thinning out now and they could catch a glimpse of the sea. In a few seconds more they would see the beach. Suddenly, they stopped. There was no need to argue further. There, practically in front of them, was the "something" of Mrs. Johnson's dream, a ship's jolly-boat or gig, stranded on the beach.

The Johnsons studied their find curiously. It was clinker-built and rigged strangely with a stubby mast and a square sail bent on a heavy spar—obviously not a Bahamian boat. The drab brown paint the British Admiralty has decreed for the lifeboats of this war was scarred and scaled by the sea. The sail was worn and tattered. In it they could see oars, canvas, buckets and other useful gear. It was unmoored and slewed sideways, just as it was left by the receding tide. A derelict, they were sure, ownerless, cast up by the sea. They pressed forward jubilantly.

A last patch of thick bush barred them from the beach. Johnson laid about him with the machete vigorously. His wife kept a pace or two behind, out of reach of the swinging blade. They were near the end of the bush now, close to the first sand of the beach.

Again Johnson stopped suddenly. His upraised machete hung suspended at the top of his stroke, then dropped slowly to his side. He stood and stared.

Some feet ahead of him, just inside the shade, lay a man—or what had been a man. Clawlike hands protruded from the remains of a uniform coat; wasted, knobby legs from what had been a pair of khaki shorts. Such parts of him as were not covered with rags or hair were burnt a deep mahogany. His head, thrown back on the sand, was a bearded skull, the cheek-bones pressing through the tight-drawn blackened skin, the closed eyes sunk in cavernous sockets. Long black locks hung down his forehead and cheeks, tangled in his ragged black beard.

Near the first man was a second, as ragged, bearded and emaciated as the first. His large nose was a ridge of cartilage and bone; his cheek-bones as salient as the other's; the rest of his face caved in. Through the tatters of what had been a pair of underwear shorts they saw his sun-burnt, withered thighs. His face, as skull-like as that of his companion, was blurred with an unkempt yellow beard. His head, twisted back convulsively, lay in a shock of bleached towlike hair, showing a corded and scraggy neck, no larger than a child's. His eyes were closed. With the fingers of his outflung pipestem arms he plucked feebly at the sand.

Both men seemed utterly spent.

The dark man's eyelids fluttered and opened slowly. Black eyes, showing a large expanse of white, glittered wildly from deep sockets overhung with shaggy brows.

"Lawd God!" Johnson exclaimed, and backed into his wife.

"Watch what you do, man!" she said crossly. Then she saw what he had seen. She clutched at him in alarm. The sea had indeed cast up her "something"—the strangest and most terrifying thing she had ever seen.

"Run," Johnson said. "We mus' fetch de Commissioner."

The Johnsons turned on their new-cut trail and ran.

It *was* a wonder from the deep that had washed up on the beach at Alabaster Bay. No strange sea monsters these but two young British seamen, scarcely more than boys, whose adventure takes its place in the first rank of the annals of the sea.

That afternoon the radio flashed the news to the world: Robert George Tapscott, nineteen, and Wilbert Roy Widdicombe, twenty-one, the sole survivors of the freighter *Anglo-Saxon,* their ship destroyed by a German raider, had crossed three thousand miles of open ocean in an eighteen-foot undecked boat, outliving seventy days of thirst, starvation and storm.

As an ordeal of endurance the classic trip of Captain Bligh and seventeen men of the *Bounty* pales in comparison. Bligh had a twenty-three foot boat, thirty-two pounds of pork, 150 pounds of bread, twenty-eight gallons of water, six quarts of rum, six bottles of wine, a quadrant, a compass, twine, canvas and cordage. At no time was he completely out of food or water. In his forty-eight-day, 3,618-mile trip from Tofoa in the South Pacific to Timor, Dutch East Indies, he landed at New Holland, where there were oysters, berries and water—again on an unnamed island, where he captured twelve noddies. Six days later his men caught a booby, and two days later, a dolphin.

The seven survivors of the *Anglo-Saxon*, three of whom were seriously wounded, had in their eighteen-foot boat one tin of ship's biscuits, eleven tins of condensed milk, three six-pound tins of boiled mutton and four gallons of water. They caught but two fish in seventy days.

The men of the *Bounty* had rations three times a day, a gill of water at each serving. The men of the *Anglo-Saxon* had rations twice a day, a ship's biscuit, a half dipper of water—about a coffee cup full—a bit of condensed milk in their evening water, and the mutton, while it lasted. In fifteen days the water was gone.

2. THE MAKING OF A SAILOR

I

TAPSCOTT

ALTHOUGH BORN within a few miles of one another, Tapscott and Wid-dicombe, whose lives were destined to be so closely linked, never met until the Lowther Lattle liner *Anglo-Saxon* sailed from Newport, England, on the last voyage she was ever to make.

Both were of West Country stock, the strain that has given England so many naval heroes and famous seamen. It has given her a great many unknown seamen as well. "Yows" the sailors call them. Bligh of the *Bounty* was a Yow. He was born at Plymouth, Devonshire, of Cornish parents.

Bob Tapscott's father, although of Devon stock, was a pilot of Cardiff, as was his father before him. There are a great many West Countrymen in maritime Wales. Cardiff is a busy port today, but it was even busier fifty years ago, when it was the main outlet for the Welsh coal mines. Pilotage was a skilled and important trade. Although he had served his time in a full-rigged ship, the *Crocodile*, John Henry Tapscott, Bob's father, chose to remain at home. He died when Bob, his youngest child, was two.

Tapscott's mother, Florence Giles Tapscott, is a Cornish woman, from the Cornish fishing town of St. Austell. Her father was in the Navy. He spent seven years in Japan as gunner's mate teaching the Japanese gunnery.

Tapscott is the youngest of a large family, four girls and two boys. He does not remember his father or either of his grandfathers. He was born in a nursing home in Bristol, May 25, 1921. His childhood was spent at Usk, an inland tow up the river from Cardiff. He had no childhood of ships and docks and sailing boats. He heard no family stories of long voyages and strange adventures, but it was in his mind to go to sea from as early as he can remember.

He attended a number of Council schools, the last one at Llysfaen, where he won a scholarship in a technical school. He was fond of soccer and swimming, and proficient at both. Later, in mid-Atlantic, he was to be profoundly thankful for his skill in swimming. Like most of the Welsh about him he sang in a church choir. He was an even-tempered, independent youngster, who went his own way. His older brother, now in the Fleet Air Arm, was six years older than he. They were too far apart in age to be very companionable.

It is no easy matter to bring up a family of six on eighteen shillings a week, plus a few shillings for each child. That is what Bob Tapscott's mother had under the Pilot's Amalgamation pension scheme. What-ever were his mother's cares, young Bob did not share them. He had no worries about the present and no great concern for the future. Today his point of view is much the same: one signs on, works hard to earn one's pay, spends it gloriously, and goes back to work again.

In 1936, when he was fifteen, his mother arranged through a sea-going friend a chance for him to go to sea without the payment of the usual premium. It was in a tramp steamer, of course. They operate with the cheapest labor. Young Bob got sixpence half-penny a day; they could afford to waive the premium,

The tramp cleared Newport for Buenos Aires with a stocky, fair-haired, gray-eyed, expectant apprentice at the rail. But a few days at sea dissipated the rosy glow of romance. He had all the dirty jobs, and couldn't even grouse about them. As lowliest in the ship, that was his lot, as it had been that of every apprentice before him. He hated the grime, grease and dirt. He loathed oiling decks in the blazing sun, a filthy wad clutched in his hand. To save refueling, the tramp carried coal on her deck which had to be moved below. For hours he lay on his stomach in the choking, black dust, slinging coal into the pockets.

A few days out and the ice-box was exhausted. There were no fresh meats or vegetables; nothing but salt beef, salt pork and beans, and finally, nothing but beans. In the eventless days of a long voyage, meals are the only thing a hungry man looks forward to, and meals and discussion of them occupy much of a seaman's conversation. The meals became smaller and worse. There was near mutiny.

Tapscott was homesick, miserable and completely disillusioned. The men were good-natured and decent enough, though they knocked him about to toughen him—or so they said. That was the system. But he grew to detest the mate. There was no pleasing him. He was a pompous bully determined to pay off the hardships of his youth on the youngest of the crew.

The change in a landsman's habit of sleep, a necessity as great to a growing youth as food, left him dazed and groggy. He couldn't adjust to watches, four hours on, four off throughout the twenty-four. He went about his duty like a somnambulist. As in a dream the mate bumbled on unceasingly: "Now, when *I* was your age . . ." until he hated him with a red hate.

Eventually they reached Buenos Aires. That was the final disillusionment. He had dreamed of shore leave in exotic ports. Here were

Robert Tapscott after his release from Nassau Hospital. *Stanley Toogood*

Wilbert Widdicombe during his convalescence. *Stanley Toogood*

different people, different speech and different scenes; but, even more than at home, he realized that the delights of a city are not much on sixpence ha'penny a day. He was signed on for a year. There was nothing he could do about it till then. At the end of three such voyages to Buenos Aires he left the tramp.

Tapscott was through with the sea; nothing was as he had imagined it. After a few days at home he hired out to a farmer. Two months of this and he was glad to sign on with a Newport tramp as mess-boy. The sea had him.

Tapscott's second job, on the *Grainton*, was good enough, except for the engineers. He had to serve them, and already he bristled with the traditional hostility between deck and engine-room. "And why not?" he asks. "Greasers take on so superior and are always telling us how much we owe them. Owe *them!* There were sailing ships and seamen before ever there were engineers."

The *Grainton* was for Cape Town to pick up mealies—cornmeal to Americans. She took twenty-six days to get there, and then they had to wait their turn for the one wharf, with a half dozen other ships. She took on ten thousand tons of mealies and sailed for Rotterdam, where the cargo was unloaded and transshipped to Germany. This was in the fall of 1937.

In Spain the curtain-raiser to World War II was being played. After a trip to Portland, Oregon, and back as a deck boy, Tapscott's next job, ordinary seaman now, was in an old ship, the *Nailsea Lass*, carrying coal and supplies to the Republicans. In addition to his better pay as seaman he had a two-hundred-per-cent bonus for time in the war zone. The skipper and mate were good sorts, and the crew congenial, including three Norwegians, who astonished even the veterans with their capacity for hard drink. There was an extra special sea-lawyer aboard, who would argue with the captain for hours. "He was stone deaf," Tapscott says, "and so was the Old Man. It was wonderful to hear 'em."

At Barcelona they had a great deal of leave. They spent long hours in the cafés, drinking strange drinks and staring at the Catalonian population and the Loyalist soldiers. Their sympathies were all with the Loyalists. They believed that if the latter could have had adequate supplies Franco never would have won.

Barcelona was full of soldiers of the International Brigade, Canadians, Americans and British. Many of them were thoroughly disgusted with the conduct of the war, particularly with the Catalonians. Like Italians, Tapscott decided, Catalonians were handy with knives and at street fighting, but when it came to the front-line variety, they were perfectly willing to let someone else do it.

The *Nailsea Lass's* crew sympathized with the English-speaking members of the Brigade. When they left Barcelona there were two of them aboard. Tapscott knew about them; he had helped escort one of them on. It had been quite simple. Five seamen arrived late at the dock gates, singing at the top of their voices and staggering convincingly. They appeared to be holding each other up. The Spanish guard shrugged contemptuously and let them through. He could not see in the semi-darkness that one of the "seamen" wore the windbreaker and khaki trousers of the Brigade. Tapscott's mates hid their Canadian in the fo'castle, while the others were disposing of a Londoner in the coal bunkers.

Steaming out of Barcelona the Old Man made a thorough inspection of the ship and routed out three stowaways. The crew were almost as surprised as he. Very angry, he ordered the ship about, but the Third Mate pleaded their cause. "After all," he said, "they're Britishers, sir, and in a bit of a fix." The Captain growled, waggled his deaf head, and finally gave in.

Tapscott was taking his trick at the wheel when he heard the Third Mate bark his name. "What do you know about this man in the fo'castle?" he demanded.

"Nothing," Tapscott said.

"The fo'castle was locked. He couldn't have got in without help. What do you know about it?"

The mate fixed him with an unrelenting eye, and Tapscott, never one to lie uselessly, told all. "But I swear," he said, "I don't know a thing about that third chap."

"Naturally," said the mate, turning away. "I stowed him myself."

The *Nailsea Lass's* next port was Valencia. She lay in harbor four days during rebel bombing. One big French ship was hit, burst into flames, and had to be beached. Tapscott was in Valencia several weeks. During severe raids the crew lived in a hotel ashore.

He would have liked to have stayed with the *Nailsea Lass,* but when the ship reached home he was paid off, together with most of the crew. It was a matter of the Captain's beer. The crew, tired of wine, strong brandies and outlandish Spanish drinks, craved honest British beer. The Captain had the only supply available. Not to put too fine a point on it, they pinched it. The Captain never could determine the exact culprits, but he had a good idea who they were. He was taking no chances on his next trip so he sacked the lot.

Tapscott was very sorry. He liked that berth.

II

WIDDICOMBE

ROY WIDDICOMBE was born at Totnes, Devonshire, April 10, 1919. His birthplace, eleven miles up the River Dart from Dartmouth, is the oldest borough town in England. His name is as Devonshire as a tor. He grew to be a sizable man, six feet tall, as dark as a gypsy. In temperament he was as unlike Tapscott as could be, impetuous, stubborn and emotional. His father, Wilbert Adam Widdicombe, a townsman of Dartmouth, and a shipyard worker there, was not of the sea. He was in the army in India during the last war, in the Wessex Artillery. He was stationed at Delhi and saw service on the Northwest Frontier. Unlike himself, Widdicombe said that his father had no taste for adventure and did not like to travel. He had been glad to return to his native town in 1919 and stay there.

Widdicombe's mother was Lily Bowhey—pronounced Booey in his native county—as Devonshire a name as Widdicombe. Her people were all farmers. She was a tall, strong, dark woman, full of energy and fond of a good time. She died when her fourth baby was ten days old. Widdicombe remembered that they were all out for a walk with the new baby when she collapsed. They took the baby from the pram and wheeled her home in it. His sister was eight at the time. Roy, four, was sent to Grandfather Widdicombe in Dartmouth. His younger brother, George, then two, went to the Bowheys in Totnes.

As happens frequently, there was some feeling between the Bowhey and Widdicombe clans. Widdicombe, while admiring and, later, emulating his father, regarded himself as all Bowhey. He missed his mother desperately and refused to accept his grandmother as surrogate. Once, when George was visiting them, he told George to pay no attention to her, saying, "She's not your proper mother," and got a "hiding" for it. There seem to have been a good many hidings. Twice he ran away to go to his mother's people. His father left the boy's upbringing entirely to the grandmother.

Dartmouth is one of the great English yachting centers. Consequently, Widdicombe was familiar with boats from as long as he could remember. From the age of six he rowed and sailed dinghies, often without the knowledge or permission of the owners. He picked up small jobs on yachts, frequently absenting himself from school to do them. He was hot-tempered and quick with his fists. The boy he fought with the most subsequently became his pal, joined the Navy, and died of pneumonia at Cape Town.

When not in trouble at school because of his truancies, Widdicombe did well; he couldn't abide anyone doing better. He won a scholarship to Grammar school, but went to the training ship *Conway* instead, ten days before his eleventh birthday. The *Conway* suited him down to the ground. She lay in the Mersey off Liverpool. Under the instruction of naval officers, 240 boys put in three years in her. The first year they had the practical side of seamanship—knots, ropes and rigs, the easier side of navigation. The second and third years they sailed boats, planned courses, worked out positions and did actual work as done aboard ship. At the end of his training, Widdicombe took the Board of Trade examination, passed, and went to sea as a deck boy.

Widdicombe's first ship was a Union Castle liner on the Cape Town run. He did not like it; it was much harder than school. His favorite school subject had been geography. South Africa was interesting and exciting. He determined to see more of the world. At fifteen, after a year with the *Union Castle*, he got his A.B.'s ticket.

Until 1934 Widdicombe was in passenger ships. He visited Australia, the United States, South America, the Mediterranean and the West Indies. He picked his berths for sun; the hotter the run the better he liked it. Cold weather depressed him and he could never get enough sun. He decided to settle down eventually in Honolulu or the South Seas. Little did he dream that one day he would cower under a stifling canvas and drench himself desperately with sea water to evade the sun's killing rays.

Nor did Widdicombe dream when he touched Nassau in the *Arandora Star* in 1937, a foot-loose sailor in what he thought a dull port, that three years later it would be the most welcome land in the world to him.

While on the *Arandora Star* at Southampton, Widdicombe and three pals in his watch conceived the bright idea of buying officers' uniforms for wear ashore. There was nothing in regulations to stop them. Widdicombe's was a third mate's; the others' an engineer's. They put them on at Alexandria and went down the gangplank under the astounded eye of the Fifth Mate. They were careful not to back them up with any claims; they had no taste to be had up for impersonation.

They were taken at their face value generally and enjoyed it thoroughly. Thereafter, ashore and at sea, the other seamen saluted them ironically and called out, "Make way for the gentlemen."

Home from that cruise, Widdicombe decided to change over to freighters. The pay was the same, but he'd have more chance to save it on a freighter. He now had a second mate's ticket. He went down to Newport to get a ship.

Swaggering up the street one evening in uniform, he came up to five giggling girls. It was dusk. He couldn't see their faces. As he passed, one called out, "Good night, Sergeant-Major." "It's a good thing we have a Navy," another added.

Widdicombe wheeled about and asked what they meant. There was more giggling, but no one answered. Seeking to impress them he asked them all to the pictures. They refused, all atwitter. He singled out one of them. "You're coming with me," he said. She refused, but added that since he was a stranger in Newport she'd show him about the town. This was Cynthia Pitman, whom he later married.

Several days at Newport, spent mostly with Cynthia, and Widdicombe was off on a tramp for South America and the canning factories of Rosario and Santa Fe. He experienced the dangerous currents of the River Plate, saw the myriads of voracious little fish that reduce a man to a skeleton in short order if he is so unfortunate as to fall in, stared at half-wild gauchos, who came to the river with cattle and hides, drank native drinks, played some football, visited the Toc H. and the Flying Angel, had the usual diversions of a British sailor in the Argentine. But he was restless and dissatisfied.

Back at Newport he looked up Cynthia immediately and decided it was the real thing.

Like Tapscott, Widdicombe was in Spain during 1938. He was in the *Stanway*, which, like the *Nailsea Lass*, was running stores to the Loyalists. The *Stanway* was just starting to unload cargo at Bilbao when the big offensive started. From there they went to Alicante, where the shaken crew got drunk. Bombing kept them on shore. There was nothing to do but make the rounds of the cafés. One shell fell a few feet from their ship. While Widdicombe was thus making the best of it at Alicante, Tapscott, at Valencia, was standing on the breakwater watching the shelling. Like Tapscott, Widdicombe had a bonus for this hazardous work.

The *Stanway* returned to Antwerp and loaded again for Alicante. Widdicombe bought American cigarettes for half a crown a carton and bartered them in Spain for silk shirts, shawls, anything. The tobacco-starved Spaniards would make any deal for cigarettes. That is how he got the suit he was married in.

3. OVERTURE TO TRAGEDY

I

WHILE BRITISH Prime Minister Neville Chamberlain was at Munich tying to stave off total war, British seaman Tapscott was back in a freighter on the Buenos Aires run. He stayed with his ship until July, when it occurred to him that what he really would like would be a passenger ship.

In the summer of 1939 he went up to London and signed on the *Atlantis* of the Royal Mail Line. She did a cruise to Helsinki, Norway, Sweden and Denmark.

On her way home the *Atlantis* passed through the Kiel Canal. There were the usual number of camera enthusiasts aboard. In spite of signs forbidding it, they took pictures freely. A Nazi guard came aboard. Without the Captain's permission, or any sort of formalities whatsoever, they seized the cameras, ripped out the film and destroyed it.

The *Atlantis* was scheduled to touch at Hamburg. She never reached it. A radio message from the owners called her home. She went straight into dry-dock. Tapscott, returning to her after four days' leave, was astonished to find her transformed into a hospital ship. It was now late August. She was ordered to Gibraltar.

September 3rd found the *Atlantis* at sea, on her way from Gibraltar to Malta. News of the declaration of war came over the radio. One of the seamen told Tapscott about it. "We're for it now," he said. Tapscott did not believe it and went to the bos'n about it. It was all too true. They were in a war.

From Malta the *Atlantis* was ordered to Alexandria. A large fleet was stationed there, waiting. Mussolini was expected to come in any minute. The *Atlantis* stood by for nine weeks, acting as a floating hospital for Army and Navy patients. She was then sent back to Southampton with fifteen insane service men as passengers.

At Southampton Tapscott was paid off. His three years' service was up. He was now an Able Seaman. He signed on a troopship at once.

Tapscott's new ship, the *Orford*, of the Orient Steam Navigation Company, was the largest ship he had yet been in—20,000 tons. She had been a fine passenger ship, and the new A.B. luxuriated in first-class cabin accommodations. She was bound for Australia to pick up the Commonwealth's first overseas contingent. She reached Freemantle, Christmas Eve, 1939, and went on to Sydney to pick up 1,500 soldiers, their equipment and a cargo of meat, grain and guns.

The *Orford* left Australia in convoy with a number of other liners. Wartime discretion prohibits details. There was a large number of warcraft present and planes circled overhead continually. The convoy touched at Colombo, steamed up the Gulf of Aden, and the *Orford* landed her troops at Ismailia, for training in Egypt. The guns and stores she discharged at Port Said.

The *Orford* never touched a British port again. From Egypt she went to Marseilles, laid up six weeks at Toulon, and thence headed for Madagascar, where she embarked 2,000 French colonials for Marseilles.

Events in Europe accelerated with dizzying speed. Back in Marseilles, Tapscott had just gone to his deluxe passenger berth, in which he slept so well, when the deck boy, beside himself with excitement, ran through the passage way, pounding on the doors.

"Shut up, you little blighter!" Tapscott roared through the closed door.

"Air raid! Air raid!" the boy yelled.

Tapscott tumbled out. He did not have to be called twice. With the others of the crew he crawled up the quay to shelter. The *Luftwaffe* came screaming down. Bombs burst all about them. Anti-aircraft banged and searchlights swept the sky. The *Orford's* crew were herded into a French Army camp for the night. When they returned to their ship, it was no more. A heavy bomb had gone right though the passenger saloon.

A special train took Tapscott and his mates to Cherbourg and a Channel steamer home. Tapscott decided to stay there a while.

II

THE WAR caught Widdicombe at sea, too. In the early days of it, he was mined. Again, exigencies of the time make it impossible to tell the whole story. His ship was lost and he was eight days at sea in a lifeboat. "But that was easy," he said. "We had plenty of food and water, warm clothes, blankets and rum."

What he remembered of this period more vividly and what in his mind was far more important was his marriage. "And that wasn't all beer and skittles either," he said. His girl's mother was against it and refused her consent. There was much palaver, heart-burnings and bitterness. In the end the ceremony was performed. Widdicombe reveled in it; he was the center of attraction. It gave him a sense of importance to be a married man. He bought a house in Newport.

Various relatives helped furnish it. Among his most prized wedding presents was a silver tea set, the gift of two Negro fishermen who had been with him on the *Stanway*. He was touched by their devotion and awed by the richness of the present.

After a round of visits to relatives in Devonshire, Widdicombe was off to sea again, this time in a ship bound for Baltimore to bring back much-needed scrap iron, steel plates and explosives. He was fully determined to quit the sea. But when he arrived home, he found that bombs had fallen on Newport, not far from his new house. Moreover, in his new capacity as family man, he needed every farthing he could find. He decided to make one more trip.

Three days later, on July 26, 1940, he signed on the *Anglo-Saxon*.

III

TAPSCOTT HAD had no intention of signing on the *Anglo*. He did it unexpectedly and with great misgiving. He had never felt that way about a ship before. He had come down to Newport to meet two pals. He was in no hurry to go to sea. They hoped to sign on a ship together. But they found it difficult to find berths for three on the same ship.

Tapscott had been in the Shipping Master's office when the Captain appealed to the Master for a man in a hurry. One of his A.B.'s had fallen ill at the last minute and he needed someone at once to take his place. Men were not easy to get. Many ships had been recommissioned; many of them were war prizes. Many seamen had been killed. The Shipping Master urged Tapscott to help him in the emergency. The ship was due to sail the following night. Reluctantly, Tapscott agreed.

From the moment he committed himself, Tapscott felt that it was a mistake. It was not because of his pals, who were disappointed that they could not all sign together. He knew nothing against the *Anglo*; he knew nothing one way or the other about her. But—he could not say why—he was full of foreboding.

The following night Tapscott and his friends had the usual pre-sailing celebration. Just after midnight, Tapscott took a taxi to the docks and went aboard.

As in most modern freighters, the *Anglo's* fo'castle was in the stern—a safety measure in case of collision. Tapscott went directly to it in the hope of getting an upper berth with a porthole. This was important, for, without a porthole, fo'castle berths were too hot for sleep in tropic latitudes. No use going on deck to sleep, either: torrential rains nearly washed one overboard.

Except for him, the *Anglo's* was a full crew, and all the good berths had been taken long since. Tapscott found an upper, but it had no porthole. He took his hard luck philosophically and stowed himself for sleep with the other ten men—eight A.B.'s and two Ordinary Seamen who slept there. In the starboard fo'castle, nine firemen slept.

Tapscott was soon asleep. He knew nothing until eleven o'clock the next morning, when he was awakened by the bos'n's order to "stand by fore and aft." The bos'n had been shouting orders all morning, but only a few of the more conscientious had turned out.

The new member of the crew made his way up the companion to the brightness of the deck. He could feel the engines pulsing and see the land and water slipping by.

The *Anglo-Saxon* was under way.

4. DEATH SHIP

THE *ANGLO-SAXON* steamed out of Newport into Barry Roads on August 5th, and dropped anchor there while the crew cleaned ship. Tapscott had opportunity to take stock of his new job and companions.

The *Anglo* was a modern flush-deck freighter, loaded with coal. Abaft the foremast was the bridge; officers' quarters on the first level; captain's quarters and boat deck above; the wheel-house and bridge proper above that; and, topping all, the railed-in square of the wheel-house roof, which houses the standard compass— "monkey island," the seamen call it. In this bridge unit were also situated the wireless room and the operators' cabins.

Amidships, about the base of the funnel, were the engineers' quarters. Aft this, at the base of the mainmast, another deck-house quartered the gunner and bos'n.

On the poop a gun platform had been erected. On this stood the tarpaulined naval gun in its turret. Between the stanchions of the gun platform was a companionway to the fo'castle below, the forward part of which was a mess room, with stove, table, benches and the lockers in which the seamen kept their clothing and mess kit.

"Not a well-deck job," Tapscott thought with satisfaction. "No running up and down ladders all the time."

Tapscott and Widdicombe found themselves in the same watch. It cannot be said that they took to each other. They quite frankly found each other uncongenial, but that was no bar to their working effectively as a watch.

Widdicombe, swarthy and swaggering, quick with his fists, would brook no opposition from anyone or anything if he could help it. He had six feet of bulk and an overwhelming confidence in himself and his abilities.

Tapscott, temperamentally as opposite as could be, is nearly as tall, five feet, eleven inches; gray-eyed and fair, with the anomaly of heavy black eyebrows. He has a slow, sweet smile, apparent docility and a strong sense of decorum.

Widdicombe thought Tapscott smug, slow and ambitionless. Tapscott found Widdicombe hasty, extravagant and unbalanced. His innermost conviction was that he was a "little touched."

The third member of the watch, Paddy Gormley, they both liked immediately. Paddy was in his thirties and had been around. He had been a soldier in the Army in India before going to sea. He would probably have been in India still, had it not been for a little matter of beating a native guard, who, ill-advisedly, persisted in reporting Paddy's and his pal's repeated absence from barracks during the night. Paddy was hard-bitten, but possessed of the Irish talent for politics and a generous share of Irish charm. He held the watch together.

These three established themselves at once as the spearhead of the fo'castle. If there was any question of work, watches, or that all-important matter to seamen, food, to be taken up with the Old Man, they did it. Others might hang back for reasons of discretion or a desire to avoid trouble. Not they!

It was over food that the fo'castle first had a sample of Widdicombe's temper. Several of them were eating at the fo'castle table. The *Anglo's* cook was Widdicombe's friend. In fact, he said, it was he who taught him to cook. "You couldn't have taught him much," Elliott, one of the A.B.'s, said. "The blighter can't boil water." Widdicombe wouldn't hear anything against the cook. One word led to another, and Widdicombe, leaping to his feet, invited the A.B. to go on deck with him. Elliott, though smaller, accepted the challenge. As he was getting to his feet, Widdicombe caught him flush in the face with his fist. He was wearing a heavy signet ring and the A.B.'s face was cut. Tapscott found this reprehensible; Widdicombe should have waited until they were on deck.

It was over food, too, that the watch got to know the cut of Captain Flynn's jib. The coffee on ship left much to be desired. "You don't know what it is," Tapscott complained. The watch agreed that they would prefer tea to this anomalous beverage and asked the steward to change to that. The steward refused. The whole fo'castle was equally indignant over the steward's conduct, but would take no action.

Paddy, Tapscott and Widdicombe went to the Captain. He received them politely, listened to their complaint, and promised to remedy the situation as soon as possible—when they next reached port, for they hadn't enough tea aboard to double the ration.

"When will that be?" they asked.

Only God, the Admiralty, the Company and the Captain knew their destination, but from the approximate date of arrival he gave them they deduced that they were bound for Buenos Aires or Bahia Blanca.

The watch reported to the fo'castle the success of their mission. Instead of being pleased, they were glum and apprehensive. They were afraid they had been compromised by the watch's officiousness. The watch decided to have nothing more to do with such poor sticks.

"Ours was a young ship," Widdicombe said. With one or two exceptions, the entire company were as young, or little older, than himself. There were forty men in all: captain; first, second and third officers; four engineers; two wireless operators; the bos'n, gunner and carpenter; ten seamen; nine firemen and two oilers; a donkey man; first and second cooks; first, second and mess-room stewards.

Of the men who were to be with them in the open boat, the Chief Mate—First Officer C. B. Denny—was the one they knew best. He was a Londoner, thirty-four years old. He was fair-haired, blue-eyed, thin and raw-boned. His jaw jutted— "Like Churchill's," Widdicombe said—and he had a brusque manner of speaking. He had been at sea all his life, and he knew his trade. He knew seamen and how to handle them. He was eminently fair and "decent." His chief diversion ashore was cycling.

The "Second Sparks," R. H. Pilcher, the watch noted, was a cut above the usual article. He, too, was a Londoner, a slight, fair and finely drawn chap, precise and gentle in speech, pleasant, uncomplaining and unfailingly polite. "A proper gentleman" was the watch's verdict; and in the minds of Tapscott and Widdicombe, a hero.

The gunner, Richard Penny, a wartime innovation aboard ship, was a gray-haired, short, stocky Devonshire man of forty-two, a veteran of the last war. He was a Royal Marine, had been wounded and was fatalistic about life and man's duration. "When your number's up, it's up," he would say in his broad Devonshire accent. Widdicombe, who was in the gun crew, tried ragging him in his own dialect and was run off the deck for his pains. Penny had separate quarters and messed apart from the men. His sole job was the operation and care of the naval gun on the poop. Good-humored and equable, he fitted in well with the life of the ship.

The Third Engineer, Leslie Hawkes, twenty-two, a short, stocky, flaxen-haired "Geordie"—Sunderland man—was making his first trip to sea.

The second cook, Leslie Morgan, twenty, was a neighbor of Widdicombe in Newport. "Lived just down the street." He was medium-sized, garrulous and at times, the watch agreed, inclined to act "silly."

The remainder of the men of the *Anglo-Saxon* were the run of the sea. Some Tapscott and Widdicombe liked; others, not. Of the latter they said nothing. "Poor chaps! They're all gone now."

The Chief Sparks, a big chap, stood out in their minds for two things; his determination to stay at sea for the rest of his life, and his declaration that he would go down with the ship, should anything happen to her.

Watches set, the gun crew organized, preparatory details of a long voyage out of the way, the *Anglo-Saxon* dropped her pilot toward sunset on August 5th and put to sea.

The ship was blacked out. Several cases of ammunition for the gun were brought up from the magazine, abaft the fo'castle, and ranged on the poop. Safety regulations were checked and rehearsed.

Tapscott and Widdicombe were assigned to the port life-boat. The ship carried two of these, capable of taking thirty men each, swung out in readiness on the davits. Rope gripes secured them. A blow with an axe or a slash with a knife and they were ready to lower. These were on either side of the boat deck above the engineers' quarters. Four life-rafts were lashed to the shrouds of the fore- and mainmasts. They were equipped with reversible lights which righted and ignited themselves automatically no matter how the raft struck the water, topside up or down. On the port and starboard sides of the bridge boat deck were two more boats, eighteen-foot jolly-boats used normally for communication between ship and shore. As a further safety measure, these, too, had been equipped with water and stores. Like the life-boats, the jolly-boats were swung out on the davits and secured with gripes.

Tapscott's and Widdicombe's orders were to go to the port jolly-boat, should their life-boat be destroyed.

Since the war is still on, it is impossible to describe details of the convoy system. But it can be said that it was no surprise to anyone when the next day they put into another English port. Here the gun that never was to fire a shot at the enemy was inspected and certified. In time and at a place that cannot be specified the *Anglo-Saxon* picked up the convoy and again put to sea.

Only the Admiralty and the Captain knew their destination. For days they steamed in line with many other ships, warcraft guarding them by water, aircraft above. Dripping fogs shrouded them. Only with the greatest difficulty could the man at the wheel follow the ship ahead. The sea was strewn with wreckage; barrels, timber, bits of gratings, shattered spars, and often bodies, some bloated to monstrosity, others far gone in dissolution.

"I'd give a hundred pounds, if I had it," said Tapscott to Paddy in the early hours of a watch, "to be out of all this. And I've never felt this way before."

One morning Tapscott went to sleep while still in convoy. When he awoke, the *Anglo-Saxon* was alone.

It was now generally known that they were bound for South America. Their course indicated this, and the Captain corroborated it when they went to complain about the shortage of tea.

Once well away from the danger zone, the weather warmed up and tension relaxed. Life aboard ship became normal. Off watch the men washed and mended their clothes or played an occasional game of cards. Mostly, they just slept.

Tapscott had a standing engagement for cribbage with one of the firemen.

5. HOLOCAUST

I

ON THE night of Wednesday, August 21, 1940, they had luncheon sausage and meatballs for tea on the *Anglo-Saxon*. The ship was making way steadily in a southwesterly direction and had left the Azores five hundred miles behind.

Widdicombe thought very little of the menu. It would be his wheel at eight o'clock, Paddy's lookout and Tapscott's stand-by. So he passed up his tea and slept instead.

Shortly before going forward, he rolled a half dozen cigarettes to take with him to the wheelhouse. It was against orders, but the *Anglo* steered like a yacht in heavy weather and like an automaton in calm. Two long hours of virtually no movement, with the binnacle paralyzing the optic nerves like a hypnotist's mirror, made it very hard for a man to keep his eyes open. Cigarettes helped.

At the stroke of the bell, Paddy went forward to his post and Widdicombe to the bridge. The Third Mate had the watch. Widdicombe checked the course with the man he relieved and settled down for his trick. The night was pitch black, with low clouds scurrying across the sky. A choppy, easterly swell buffeted the *Anglo* on the port bow, but she wallowed imperturbably on.

Tapscott, in the mess-room forward of the port fo'castle, was engrossed in a four-handed game of cribbage with a fireman and two A.B.'s. He should have been amidships for his stand-by, but he wanted to finish the game. He had the crib, but had not yet discarded. He noted his hand with elation: a high count, two sevens, an eight and a nine. And he had not yet looked in the crib! There was a cup of tea at his elbow and some bacon he had saved from his breakfast.

Elliott, one of the A.B.'s his watch had just relieved, was ragging Tapscott.

"The mate's been whistling for you," he said.

Tapscott studied his hand. He did not believe him. He was in no hurry to go on deck.

"Better look slippy," Elliott added. "He's blowing his brains out."

"Eh?" said Tapscott, looking up. Elliott's face was guileless. "Hell," Tapscott added regretfully, and got up from the table. As he started for the companionway, Elliott went after him and pulled him back.

"Sit down," he said with triumph, "I was 'aving you."

Tapscott, grinning sheepishly, went back to his game.

A rending crash in the firemen's fo'castle brought the players to their feet. Four explosions, so close together that they seemed one, shook the ship from stern to stem. The men stared at one another, the dreaded question in their eyes: mine or torpedo?

The fireman was first to move. He threw down his cards and bolted for the companionway. Tapscott and the others ran to their lockers and snatched their life-belts. Struggling into them, they followed the fireman up the steps, Tapscott in the lead.

As he reached deck, a blinding glare struck Tapscott like a blow in the eyes. It lighted up the fireman's back against the curtain of blackness in front of them. The fireman plunged forward. Tapscott had only one idea: he must not lose sight of that back. He sprang after the fireman, struggled for balance, and the whole world seemed to blow up behind him in one terrific roar and shocking blast. He felt himself fly through the air and crash into something hard; then he knew nothing.

Tapscott came to on the starboard side of the deck twenty feet from the companionway. He was flat on his face, his nose jammed against the deckhouse bulkhead. He tried to move, but his muscles refused. He felt no pain—nothing at all. He wondered if he were dead. He lay there for what seemed a long time. Actually, it was only a few seconds.

Of a sudden, life flowed back into Tapscott's legs. He staggered to his feet and propped himself against the bulkhead. He weaved for a moment like a drunken man and started forward, stumbling and reeling. Something was splattering overhead with leaden thuds. He stared upward. The night was full of whizzing, incandescent streaks, some close to him, going so fast they seemed to merge into continuous lines. Machine-gun bullets! Incendiaries! He threw himself flat on his face.

Lying there, Tapscott wondered dully what was happening. It never occurred to him that the ship was being shelled. Who was doing this? And why? What matter who was doing it? Those red, white, and blue streaks were all that mattered now. Suddenly they ceased. He jumped up and ran for the engineers' quarters.

Running, Tapscott knew he had been hurt; but where? How? By what? He felt no pain, only numbness. And he could not move fast enough. He drove his flagging body by an effort of will. He *must* get across the open deck to the shelter of the engineers' deckhouse.

The firing started again. Tapscott flung himself down and crawled frantically toward his objective. This time it was the incessant bang-bang of pom-poms. He closed his eyes and tried to shut his ears against them, lying still and pressing himself as flat as he could against the pates of the deck. He was aware that someone was crouching beside him; who, he did not know. The din was deafening.

The metal storm moved forward. Tapscott dived into the engineers' alleyway. Two men were coming toward him in the gloom, one carrying an electric torch pointed down. Tapscott rushed past them out of the alleyway and on to the covered hatch. He dropped on all fours and scrambled across the hatch cover to the port side of the ship. It was a desperate chance. Pom-pom shells flashed and banged. Incendiary bullets played across the deck in streams.

He reached the lee of the bridge and crouched there, spent and panting. Another man was there, the gunner, Penny. A pom-pom burst near them like a small exploding sun, and Penny grunted, shot through the wrist. Machine-gun bullets splattered over them; a few at first, then a steady hail. The two men threw themselves on their faces.

Tapscott's head was on Penny's shoulder. He could feel the bulk of his life-belt against his body; and something moist and pulpy plastered to his neck—something "not my own." His shirt clung wetly to him, and the deck underneath was slimy. Flying metal hammered against metal; the ship was full of its clangor. Underneath roared a torrent of chaotic sounds punctuated by detonating shocks and crashes.

Penny groaned in Tapscott's ear, long, shuddering groans that forced his clenched teeth apart. A piece of shrapnel had torn through his thigh. Penny had been wounded in the last war and knew what it meant. He prayed, he told Tapscott later, that a bullet would finish him.

Tapscott knew now that his own back was bleeding. Fragments of the shell that had blasted him across deck were lodged there. That was his own blood saturating his shirt, but the pool underneath was not. Groping with the tips of the fingers of his outstretched hands he encountered the limp, torn body of a man. Paddy, probably; he had been the only one forward.

Feet trampled overhead. Tapscott could distinguish voices in a lull in the general noise. Tackle creaked. Someone was lowering a jolly-boat! A second later the boat appeared with a run, bow down. It stopped with a jerk and hung there at an angle of forty-five degrees.

Tapscott and Penny scrambled to their feet. The whole boat was in view now, lowering smoothly. Penny hauled himself over the bulwark and rolled into it. Tapscott half vaulted and half dived after him. He landed flush on the sprawled-out gunner. Penny groaned.

II

IT WAS 8:20 when the first salvo from the raider plowed into the *Anglo-Saxon's* poop, demolishing the gun and killing everyone in the starboard fo'castle. Widdicombe knew the time to the tick, for he had just glanced at the wheelhouse clock and noted with satisfaction that twenty minutes of his trick was behind him.

A tearing crash and explosions shook the ship. Widdicombe ran out of the wheelhouse to the port end of the bridge. He could see nothing—only blackness and the water alongside. He ran back across the bridge to the starboard end and peered over the weather cloth. About a quarter of a mile away a dark shape was racing obliquely toward them, gun flashes stabbing from her as she came.

A raider!

Widdicombe tore back to the wheel and put it hard aport.

The hail of lead and steel that was pouring into the ship aft moved forward. It cut through the *Anglo's* upper works with machine-like precision. It dropped to deck level and raked her fore and aft.

A breastwork of concrete building blocks protected the wheelhouse. Bullets were hammering into it. Shell fragments and shrapnel tore the ship all along the starboard side. Incendiary bullets crisscrossed into her in burning lines.

The Third Mate, whom Widdicombe had been unable to find, ran in from the bridge.

"Put her hard aport," he yelled.

"She's hard aport now," Widdicombe yelled back.

The Third dived into the shelter of the breastwork. The noise of destruction rose to a crescendo.

"I'm going for orders," the Third called, making for the inside companionway. Widdicombe, jamming the wheel to port, saw him disappear. He never saw him again.

Holding hard on the wheel, Widdicombe saw that his hands were wet with sweat. He shivered like a nervous horse. The ship was blazing in a dozen places and the noise was deafening. He could stand it no longer. He left the wheel and ran out on the bridge again.

The raider was within a hundred yards now. Widdicombe could see her clearly. She was firing with everything she had. A red glow lighted up the *Anglo's* poop. The starboard life-boat was burning; the jolly-boat on that side was smashed.

Widdicombe looked directly below. A body was slumped against the bulwark, just outside the Captain's quarters. It was Captain Flynn's. A machine-gun burst had caught him full in the chest as he was dumping the ship's papers overboard.

The storm of fire was moving forward again. Widdicombe ran back to the wheel. The First Mate was coming up the port ladder two steps at a time, followed by the Chief Sparks.

"Antennas are all shot away and sets smashed, sir," the Chief Sparks said. "No hope of an S.O.S. now."

"Right," said the Mate. "Hold her where she is," he ordered Widdicombe. "I'll be back in a minute."

The Mate went below, down the inside companionway. Huddled near Widdicombe in the shelter of the concrete-block breastwork, the Chief Sparks leaned over and shouted: "I know where there's a drink. Let's go get it." He grinned invitingly.

Widdicombe shook his head violently and clung to the wheel. His eyes were rolling, showing the whites.

The Chief Sparks went down the ladder to the steward's pantry below, where the spirit locker was. He reappeared a minute or two later brandishing a large bottle of rum from which he had already taken a big swig. "Come on," he yelled, starting for the port ladder and beckoning Widdicombe on with the bottle.

But Widdicombe stayed where he was. The Chief Sparks disappeared down the ladder. It seemed an hour since the attack had begun. By the clock, Widdicombe saw, only six minutes had elapsed.

The Mate returned to the bridge. "The Captain's gone," he said. "Bear a hand. I'm going to get the port boat away."

Widdicombe left the wheel and followed the Mate. They ran to the port jolly-boat, the Mate fumbling for his knife as he ran. He got the knife opened and sawed at the ropes of the gripes. It seemed incredible to Widdicombe that they could be so tough and resistant.

Widdicombe stood by the after-fall. As the Mate's knife bit into the last strands of the gripe the boat went down with a run. The after-fall fouled round Widdicombe's body, pulling his hand into the block and jamming it there. The whipping rope stripped his trousers from his hips and seared his arm as it went. The boat hung by the stern.

Working frantically and in great pain from his jammed hand, Widdicombe managed to clear the block. The Mate leveled the boat and they lowered away. As it passed the deck below, two men leaped into it.

III

IN BOAT drill it was Tapscott's routine job to fend off. Automatically, after falling into the dropping jolly-boat, he found the boat hook and held it off the *Anglo's* side. The boat settled smoothly into the sea, rising and falling with the brisk swell. It was also his job to unhook the forward fall. He did this and then realized that there was no one to free the after-fall. He clambered over the hapless Penny, cast off, and went forward again to stand by the boat rope.

The Chief Mate was first down the lifeline. He slid so rapidly that the skin of his fingers and palms was badly burned. Widdicombe was next. As he swung off the ship, the Second Sparks came running up. He had on a hat and carried a sweater and an attaché case. "Wait for me," he begged.

A moment later the Second Sparks came down the lifeline, just in time. Tapscott took only one turn of the boat rope—which is fastened fore and aft from ship to boat. Having reckoned without the fact that the ship was going full speed ahead, the rope ripped through his hands, burning and lacerating them when he tried to hold fast. The jolly-boat went rapidly astern.

It was Widdicombe's job, too, to fend off. He and Tapscott attacked it with the energy of fear. The *Anglo's* propeller, churning powerfully, was drawing them into the stern. The easterly swell made it difficult to keep away from the ship. One touch of the whirling blades and all would be over.

As they swept by amidships, the men in the jolly-boat saw the smashed life-boat over them and faces peering down. Two of the men overhead dropped into the boat. Tapscott and Widdicombe, frantically plying boat hook and oar, did not even see them. They gave two last mighty shoves against the ship's side and the boat swept around the stern, clearing the propeller by inches.

The *Anglo's* poop was ablaze now and the raider was closing in to finish her. The men in the jolly-boat crouched like hunted animals and scarcely breathed. The swell was carrying them right across the raider's bows. They waited for a burst from her guns.

The jolly-boat went by within a scarce hundred feet of the raider. She was blacked out; but arcs of incendiary bullets played overhead and her silhouette was clear against the lightening sky. "The *Weser*," Widdicombe said to himself. He had seen her before in the River Plate.

It seemed impossible that they would not be discovered. But the raider was so intent on the kill, she hung on the *Anglo's* blazing trail.

Hunter and hunted rushed ahead. The jolly-boat drifted away on the swell. The boat was taking water badly but the men in her dared not move. When they were a good half mile astern they put out their oars, headed the boat into the sea and pulled.

Tapscott and Hawkes were on one thwart; Widdicombe and Penny on the other. Hawkes pulled excitedly at his oar. "Pull," he exhorted Tapscott. "Harder. You're not pulling hard enough."

"What d'ye think I am," Tapscott, who was pulling his best, shot back, "a bloody reciprocating engine?"

"None of that," growled the Mate. "Pipe down and row."

They settled into their swing and made the boat leap. They were congratulating themselves on making good progress in their escape when, dead ahead, the moon rose, flooding the sea with brightness and throwing them into sharp relief. The men froze on their oars and swore.

"Don't move more than you have to," the Mate said. "Just keep her into the swell."

In their nervousness three of the men lighted cigarettes. The Mate swore. Starting guiltily, they quickly dropped them into the sea.

Water had been coming over the side. After heading the boat to the swell there should not have been as much of it as there was. It was now slopping about their calves.

"That drainage plug must be loose," Tapscott said. No one paid any attention.

Widdicombe and Tapscott seized bailers and attacked the rising water. Pilcher and Morgan relieved them at the oars. But bail as fast as they could, the water did not lower as it should. The Mate plunged his arm into it and groped along the bottom of the boat. He found the drainage plug. Tapscott had been right; the plug was half out of the hole and water coming in around it. He drove it in with his axe and they were able to get the water down to the level of their ankles.

Between the boat and the *Anglo*, lights suddenly appeared bobbing up and down on the crests of the waves. "The life-rafts!" exclaimed the men in the boat. The Mate tried to signal them with his torch; but, fearing the raider would see them, he stopped. They put the boat about and rowed toward the rafts. As they neared them, the raider swung its guns, and streams of incendiary bullets poured into them. On the rise of the next swell, the men in the boat saw, the bobbing lights were gone. The life rafts and the men clinging to them had been obliterated.

The white finger of a searchlight reached out from the raider and swept the stricken *Anglo-Saxon* from bow to stern. In its brilliance the men in the boat saw the pom-poms riddling her funnel. Streams of incendiary bullets played on the wreckage of the wireless room; no one was to survive to send a message.

At nine o'clock by the Mate's wrist watch an explosion rent the *Anglo's* poop, followed, five minutes later, by another. "The magazines," said the men in the boat. Their ship's bow was rising now. When almost perpendicular, it snapped back with a jerk and she went down by the stern. There was a great hissing as the water reached her fires, and a cloud of steam shot up from her. It took less than a minute. The waves closed over her. Only a pall of black steam overhead remained to mark where she had been. The men in the boat watched silently. Even Morgan, the garrulous, had nothing to say. "It's a terrible thing," Tapscott thought, "to see your ship go down."

The raider, her work of destruction over, headed off into the east.

"Well," said the Mate some time later, rousing himself from the general apathy, "we'd best lie to for the night. There's a sea-anchor under the forward thwart. Bend a line on it and get it over."

Tapscott and Widdicombe rigged the drogue and paid out the line. It brought the bows of the jolly-boat into the sea but was not large enough to enable them to dispense with the oars altogether.

"Right," said the Mate, when he saw how matters stood. "We'll have to stand watches. Tapscott and Widdicombe will take the first. Keep her head into it or we're liable to swamp."

Changing places, Pilcher groaned.

"What's the matter?" the Mate asked.

"My foot. I think it's blown off."

"It can't be as bad as that. How could you have rowed? I'll take a look at it."

The Mate flashed his torch. The bottom of the boat was awash with bloody water and was full of the smell of blood. Tapscott's seat was smeared with it, from the shrapnel wounds in his back.

"You've been hit, right enough," said the Mate, straightening up, "but you still have a foot. I'll dress it for you in the morning. . . . Everybody try to get some sleep now."

The Mate and Hawkes stretched themselves on the side seats. Penny and Pilcher lay in the stern. Morgan had collapsed in the bow sheets. Tapscott and Widdicombe, on the thwarts, pulled and backed with the running swells. The boat swung giddily at her sea-anchor and heaved sickeningly up and down. Pilcher and Penny started to retch.

"Not sick are you, Sparks?" said the Mate, banteringly. "I thought you were a trawler man."

Pilcher only groaned and retched distressingly.

Someone, half ironically, started to sing "Roll Out the Barrel."

"Stow it," the Mate ordered, sharply. "Sound carries over water and those swine may be somewhere about."

The singing stopped.

No one could sleep; they were too cold, wet and miserable. The swell pounded the boat and the spray rained down in clouds. At midnight the Mate and Hawkes relieved the two A.B.'s. Tapscott and Widdicombe lay down where Hawkes and Denny had been, but could sleep no better than the rest. In the end they all gave it up and talked in lowered voices.

"To think," said the Mate, shivering in his uniform of white cotton drill, "I changed to whites only this morning. And I left everything in the pockets of my blues. Stuff we could use."

But in spite of their uncomfortable situation they were not down-hearted. They all believed they would be picked up the next day. There was no good reason for believing this, but they did not think that far. They had escaped the raider and rescue was sure to follow.

"Even if we're not picked up right away," the Mate said, confidently, "we're only a thousand miles from land. And we can make that easily." He must have known better; but it cheered them to hear him say it.

No one spoke of the ship or the men that were gone. No one could speak of that just then. They were only now beginning to realize exactly what had happened, what it meant. As the early morning hours dragged on, talk stopped altogether.

The sun rose at six o'clock on seven cold, sad, wet and thoroughly miserable men. As the long level rays lighted up the surface of the sea and a golden light flooded the sky, with one accord all who could stood up and scanned the sea. In all that tossing circular plane they could see nothing, nothing save empty miles of water, nothing on the surface of the ocean and nothing in the sky. They were completely and singularly alone.

6. OPEN BOAT

"WELL," SAID the Mate, briskly, when he had satisfied himself that there was nothing human to be seen in the whole circle of the sea, "the sooner we start, the sooner we'll be there."

"Be where?" the men asked.

"The Leeward Islands," the Mate said. "There's no use going east. Wind and current are against us. Finding the Azores would be like looking for a needle in a haystack."

"Yes," said Widdicombe, "but supposing we miss the Leeward Islands?"

"Even if we sail right through them," the Mate said, "there is the Caribbean and the whole coast of North and South America."

The men were content to abide by the Mate's decision. "Clean up a bit now and we'll get going," he said. "The Third and I will take the first watch." The swell had ironed out considerably in the early hours of the morning. The warmth of the mounting sun relaxed their chill wet bodies. Everyone turned to with a will. Several even attempted mild jokes. All had been so profoundly shaken by what had happened to them they did not even think of food and drink.

Pilcher's wounded leg had stiffened so that it stood out straight before him. In daylight they saw that he was much more badly wounded than he had led them to believe. Shrapnel or a dum-dum bullet had torn through the length of his left foot, reducing it to a pulp of tissue and shattered bone. The men marveled that he could have rowed as he did in the first hours of their flight from the ship. "I didn't feel it," he said deprecatingly. They moved him forward into the bow-sheets, fashioning a sling from his scarf to keep his stiff leg from moving with the motion of the boat.

The gunner, Penny, had a badly torn hip, where shrapnel had caught him as he ran across the *Anglo-Saxon's* deck. The bullet that had gone through his right forearm as he lay with Tapscott in the shelter of the bridge had left a hole, comparatively clean. Both wounds being on his right side, they arranged the gunner forward on his left, bolstering him as best they could against the roll.

Morgan, the second cook, had a jagged tear just above his right ankle, where shrapnel or flying metal of some variety had caught him as he scrambled to the boat. His whole foot was bruised and swollen. He had a badly contused hand as well.

Tapscott had the Mate check him up for wounds. One of his front teeth, which had been broken off, exposing the nerve, when he was hurled through the air by the explosion of a shell, was now paining him considerably, but blood had stopped seeping down his back. The Mate found that a small piece of shrapnel had buried itself in Tapscott's left buttock, another in the muscles of his back and another in the palm of his left hand. A long splinter, evidently spent, had gone through his shorts into his right groin. It had burned him painfully but had not penetrated his flesh.

The wounded men disposed of, the able men got in the sea-anchor, stepped the stubby mast they found in the boat and set sail. They headed the boat due west to make west-southwest, a note on the compass advising them that it was out several points. A good breeze was blowing from the east. They were on their way to shelter and safety, they felt, doing all of four knots.

With the boat bowling along at a pleasurable clip and the sun warming them, the survivors of the *Anglo-Saxon* became almost gay. Morgan recovered his voice and chattered and sang from where he lay in the bow. His favorite song was a popular music hall number which insisted that "only one in a million will ever complain."

Sparks had a few cigarettes in his case; the Mate found several in his pockets; and Widdicombe still had some left from the supply he had rolled for consumption during his trick at the wheel. Everyone had a smoke.

They took stock of the boat and supplies. The boat, eighteen feet long and six wide, was stoutly built and in sound condition. Seats ran fore and aft on either side inboard, converging at the bow. These were rounded off at the stern to join a roomy seat across it, underneath which was a locker. Two stout thwarts completed the seating arrangements.

The boat was propelled by a dipping lug, a powerful sail in the hands of experts. It was large enough to carry the boat along at decent speed but not so large as to be dangerous in squally weather. It is the favorite rig of fishermen and trawlers on the English coast. It has the disadvantage, however, of having to be lowered every time the boat is tacked, no maneuver for amateurs. This is the only way the spar from which it is suspended can be passed to the other side of the mast. Hence the name.

For equipment there was a sea-anchor, a boat hook, six pairs of oars, a steering oar, an axe, the Mate's knife, two bailers, a rope painter, the boat's canvas cover, badly worn and torn, and a few ends of rope. In the locker under the stern seat was a boat's compass, a colza oil lamp with a bucket large enough to hold it—this for signaling in Morse—a dozen red flares in watertight canisters, a dozen matches in a water-tight container and a medical kit.

Further to equip it as a life-boat, three air-tight tanks had been built into it; one in the bow, and two on either side in the middle; and a lifeline within easy reach from the surface of the sea fixed along both of the boat's sides.

Food supplies consisted of three tins of boiled mutton, weighing six pounds each; eleven tins of condensed milk and thirty-two pounds of ship's biscuit in an air-tight metal tank fixed forward under the first thwart. Behind this was the water breaker, a keg in a cradle, with a wide bung in the top, and two long-handled, narrow mouthed dippers for scooping up its contents.

Only Sparks had been able to bring anything away from the ship. In his attaché case he had a Rolls razor, a half pound of Capstan rough smoking tobacco, a half pound of Capstan medium fine, a pipe, his trawler discharge book, his wallet, his operator's log and time sheets, and a book of Bible quotations. There was one for every day of the year. Neither Tapscott nor Widdicombe ever knew who was the compiler of this collection. They were glad to have these sheets for cigarette paper and always read the "motto" before absorbing it in smoke. All of the seamen had had cases like Sparks' packed against emergency, but none had been able to reach them.

Sparks, too, was the best-dressed man in the boat, which is to say he had the most clothes. He had a cap, uniform coat, shirt, shorts, shoes and underwear. He had, too, a sweater and a scarf.

The Mate had underwear and whites. He had no hat, but did have a particularly fine pair of shoes, white buckskin now stained with salt water. He was very annoyed about that. "And you couldn't blame him," Tapscott says; "they must have cost all of two quid."

Tapscott had, in addition to his underwear, khaki shorts, a singlet, heavy knitted Air Force socks and heavy shoes. Widdicombe had underwear, a pair of tattered trousers and a cotton shirt. Penny wore the khaki shirt and trousers of the Marine undress uniform. Morgan had denim cook's trousers and a singlet.

The sun was now high enough to shine down hotly. The men took off their soaked clothing and spread it dry.

The Mate made himself a log book with the back of Sparks' time sheets. For calendar he cut a notch in the port gunwale, the first in his record of days. In his log he wrote:

> *August 21st, 1940. At 8:20 p.m. in Lat. 26: 10 N. Long: 34.09 W. attacked by German raider presumed to be S.S.* Weber *or* Weser, Hamburg American Line. *Vessel not sighted until she had steamed within a mile of us. Pitch-black night. First sent four shells four inch crashing into poop and gun platform aft. Many of crew in fo'castle were killed. She steamed to within three cables and raked the deck with incendiary machine-gun bullets colored red, yellow, white and blue. Then a shell hit engine room starboard side and main boiler burst. The bridge and wireless room were raked with pom-pom shells and machine-gun bullets. Some of the crew went to boat decks but were mowed down by machine-gun fire. The two big boats were badly damaged. Senior wireless operator reported wireless installation smashed, unable to send S.O.S. On reporting to Master found him presumed shot down by machine-gun bullets in his cabin. Saloon amidships was wrecked. Poop by this time was blazing and the crew, few in number, were told to take to the boats. The port gig under my orders was lowered and contained seven of the crew, comprising Chief Officer C. B. Denny, 3rd. Engineer H. L. Hawkes, 2nd. W/T Officer R. H. Pilcher, A. B. Widdicombe, W. R. A. B. Tapscott, R. G., Gunlayer F. Penny, Assistant Cook*

L. Morgan, of whom the second operator was badly injured in the left foot by gunfire and 2nd cook in right foot, while gun-layer was shot through right forearm and right leg. When gig pulled away from the vessel the raider was lying off a half mile to port and a few minutes later fired tracer bullets into two life rafts launched from vessel. The vessel sunk stern first and shortly disappeared altogether. Raider headed off to eastward. Assumed that Germans wanted no members of crew left alive and were fortunate in this boat's crew escaping observation. We lay hove to all night with sea anchor out and at dawn could see no trace of any description. Having no instruments for navigation except boat's compass we set sail dipping lug and course started west to make W.S.W. true, trusting to God's good grace to either finding a vessel en route or striking somewhere in the Caribbean Sea.

Routine having been established, the Mate opened the medical kit. It consisted of a bottle of iodine, two rolls of bandage, a packet of medical lint and a pair of scissors. "Just the thing for taking to a picnic in the New Forest!" he said, on seeing the size of it. There were several rubber finger cots in the kit. He put these on his fingers that had been burned sliding down the life line from the ship; they were now raw and painful.

Sparks was treated first. With the aid of the Third Mate and Tapscott, the Mate bathed Sparks' mangled foot in sea-water and cleaned it as best he could. On close examination it seemed crushed beyond any hope of saving; the shattered bone protruded through a bloody pulp.

"Man," said the Mate, shaking his head, "how could you have pulled a boat with a foot like that?"

"It wasn't anything," Sparks said. "I tell you I didn't feel it."

"If we were in port I am afraid the doctor would have it off," the Mate said.

Sparks was silent. Fever was already coursing through his depleted veins; he had lost a great deal of blood. "I know we must be careful with the water," he said; "but do you think that I might have a drop? Just enough to wet my throat."

They gave him a drink. It was then that the Mate discovered that the water breaker had lost some of its contents; it was little over half full—about four gallons.

After sterilizing and binding up the wounds of the injured men and settling them as comfortably as they could, the able men bailed the boat, made ready the life-boat lamp and set up as orderly a routine as possible in quarters so cramped.

The Mate returned to his log and wrote:

Thursday, August 22nd, 1940. Wind N.E. 3, slight sea, slightly confused easterly swell. Course by compass W. All's well. Medical treatment given.

During the long afternoon they dozed, chatted, did puzzles, asked each other silly conundrums and speculated on the rate of speed they were making. They checked up their experiences of the night before and tried to establish the fate of the others in the ship.

Morgan had been lying in his berth in his quarters on the port side of the ship when the attack struck. He was listening to a small radio set. A shell passed clean through his cabin from starboard to port carrying the radio set with it. He ran to the saloon, where he encountered the steward. Together they started for the starboard life-boat, when the hail of machine-gun bullets moved up the deck. The steward went down under it but Morgan reached the boat deck unharmed. He found the bos'n there.

A new stream of fire smashed the boat and killed some men coming up to it.

He could not recognize the men. He and the bos'n scrambled frantically across the engine room skylight to port, going on all fours.

Halfway across, a bullet killed the bos'n. From the port boat deck Morgan saw that the life-boat was damaged beyond use and the jolly-boat coming sternward along the ship's side. He dropped to the deck below and from it into the boat. How or where he had received his wound he did not know. His hand he had hurt, he was sure, in dropping into the boat.

Pilcher had been asleep in his berth when the first salvo shattered the ship's poop. He pulled on his clothes, seized his attaché case, and rushed out on deck. He set out for the starboard life-boat. Pom-poms were bursting all about him and incendiary bullets sweeping the deck. He reached the boat and found it riddled and smoldering. He ran across to the port life-boat. It, too, was beyond use. He ran down to the deck and forward to the shelter of the bridge. As he reached it he saw that the jolly-boat had been lowered and Widdicombe going over the side. He swung on to the lifeline and followed.

Hawkes, too, had been asleep in his berth in the engineers' quarters. His cabin was on the inside of the engineers' alleyway. There were two thicknesses of steel bulkhead between him and the attack. He ran up to the boat deck and into a storm of flying metal and exploding shells. He saw the life-boat blazing and ran to the port side through the worst of the shelling. Like Morgan, he dropped to the deck and from there into the jolly-boat when it came abreast.

The Mate had been in his cabin on the port side of the bridge deck-house when the raider opened fire. He went immediately to the Captain's quarters to report. But in that brief time the machine-guns had done their work. He found the Captain dead. He went aft to examine the condition of the ship. It was the Mate Tapscott had seen with the electric torch. When the Mate was certain that there was no hope of saving the ship, that only a few of the crew were left, he ordered them to the boats. He estimated that all this had taken not more than ten minutes, more probably six.

The men in the jolly-boat had their first rations that evening at six: a ship's biscuit apiece. No one asked for water. As night fell the wounded and the men off watch made themselves as comfortable as they could under the tattered boat cover. It kept off some of the spray.

When they came to light the small colza oil binnacle lamp—the compass was housed in a hoodlike affair of metal with the lamp fixed inside—they could not get it to ignite. They tried to light the large lam with no better success.

"Too bad," said the Mate. "We'll have to steer by the stars."

They changed watches regularly during the night. The wind held and the boat ran before it, taking water now and then, which was promptly bailed out by the man on stand-by.

Everyone got some sleep. Those who could not sleep lay quietly. Now and again, one of the wounded men groaned in spite of himself. Underneath the canvas, someone snored.

Tapscott shifted about on his hard plank bed, trying to settle his hip bone so as to give him some ease. The boat was sailing handily. Seas struck it sharply and ran hissing by. Occasionally it rose on the crest of a wave and dropped with a booming shock that vibrated its timbers and sent a cloud of spray raining down on them.

"How odd," Tapscott thought, "to be out in the middle of the ocean in a boat as small as this!" He glimpsed in his mind's eye for a brief moment the immensity of the sea. He thought of the power for disaster that lay under even its most pleasant aspects and his mind turned hurriedly away.

The war, of course, was to blame. But in a war far worse things could happen to a man. Worse things had already happened to a lot of them. Poor Paddy! Why couldn't he have been one of those saved? Suddenly, Tapscott was profoundly thankful, thankful to be there at all.

Something of this was in everyone's mind. They said nothing of their danger and discomfort. They were alive. That was enough. And they were confident that within fifteen days—perhaps sooner if a ship picked them up—they would be touching foot to solid land.

7. COURSE BY COMPASS WEST

AT SUN-UP the next day the men in the boat had their first water since the sinking of the *Anglo-Saxon*. Everyone was thirsty with the normal thirst of a man who has been without water for some time.

The Mate had considered their chances of making land, the minimum food and water that would sustain life, and the amount of it they had in the boat. He set half a dipper of water, morning and evening, a little of the condensed milk with it, and half a biscuit, morning and evening, as their daily ration.

Everyone was hungry now, but not unduly so.

"If I'd known what we were getting into," Widdicombe said, "I wouldn't have passed up tea night before last. Every time I think of that sausage and mashed I'm fair narked."

The wounded men appreciated the water the most. They were feverish, but uncomplaining.

"Worth a guinea a box," said Penny as he smacked his lips over it. Everyone laughed; he was quoting the advertising slogan of a well-known brand of proprietary liver pills.

The wind was east-northeast; the sea still running an easterly swell. They were not shipping as much water as before. The boat was leaking, but not enough to cause alarm. They decided a splinter of shrapnel must have reached her somewhere forward. Just where they could not determine.

The day passed uneventfully. Everyone's spirits were good, but conversation lagged. They had worn out their slim stock of conundrums. The sun was warm but not in the least oppressive. The wounded and the men off watch slept a good deal. It was not unlike their routine aboard ship where sleep occupied most of their time off duty.

Physical functions practically ceased; their bodies had no waste to eliminate.

At six in the evening they had their biscuit and half dipper of water, changed the watch, and settled down for the night. They knew by this time every bolt head, rib, knot and protuberance of the boat's planking. They had learned, too, how to dodge spray so as to get the minimum wetting. Under the tattered boat cover they were out of the wind and most of the wet; the night was appreciably warmer; they enjoyed good hours of sleep.

Tapscott and Widdicombe had finished their watch at ten o'clock and had turned in when they were awakened by a stir within the boat. It was eleven o'clock by Widdicombe's wrist watch, which was still functioning.

"What is it?" they asked, sleepily.

"Ship," said the Mate, fumbling hastily in the locker under the stern seat.

"Where?" they demanded, wide awake now and straining their eyes into the surrounding darkness.

The whole boat awoke and sat up eagerly trying to see.

"Aft," said Hawkes, who had the stand-by.

The Mate was unscrewing the top of the container that held the flares. As their eyes adjusted themselves to the light they saw a ship in outline heading north-northeast. She was blacked-out; but they could see her clearly.

The Mate extracted a flare, struck it on the milled top of the container and held it, spluttering and hissing, over his head. The boat and the sea for yards around were lighted up with a dazzling red glare. They sat silent while the flare burnt itself out. When the last bead of the chemical composing it had melted, flamed, charred and gone out, the night closed in, blacker than before. The Mate flung the smoking stick into the sea. They brought the boat into the wind and waited.

When they could again see, the ship had turned and was coming back to them in a wide circle, as if afraid of a trap. They started to cheer. The Mate silenced them curtly. As she swung around they could see what he feared. Her build was German, or, at least, very like a German.

"I don't like the looks of her," said the Mate.

The stranger was now almost opposite them.

"Lower the sail," the Mate ordered. They dropped the dipping lug and lay to.

"If she's British she will put a searchlight on us," Widdicombe said.

"Stow it," the Mate said, "and lie low."

They crouched down in the boat and waited while the stranger hung off to the starboard.

"A Jerry, or I'm a Chinaman," said the Mate. "Look at the way she acts."

They waited there, their hearts stepping up to a higher beat. After some minutes of cruising at slow speed the stranger turned, gathered speed and made off to the north-northeast.

"We're damn well out of that," said the Mate.

Perhaps they were; but, at the same time, they felt distinctly let down. It was not right of fate to send them succor and then to snatch it away. So new were they to the open boat, however, and so little experienced in this kind of hardship, that they soon forgot their disappointment and returned confidently to their original design: they would make a friendly shore within fifteen days and all these fears and discomforts would be forgotten. They hoisted sail and resumed their course: west by compass.

The next morning, after dealing out the early ration, the Mate cut another notch of his toll of days in the gunwale and wrote up his log for the previous one.

> *August 23rd. Friday. Wind E.N.E. 3, slight sea, slightly con-*
> *fused easterly swell, partly cloudy. Half a dipper of water per*
> *man 6 a.m. Also half a biscuit with a little condensed milk.*
> *Sighted a vessel showing no lights at 11 p.m. showed sea flare,*
> *she cruised around but was of the opinion she was raider as she*
> *was heading N.N.E. We were about a hundred miles from our*
> *original position. Kept quiet let her go off.*

Saturday passed without incident. While everyone was cheerful enough, there were long periods of silence. The wind had hauled around to the northwest; the sky was cloudy. The Mate peered anxiously into the bung of the water breaker and noted the lowering level. He wrote in his log:

> *August 24th. Saturday. Crew's spirits cheerful, wind N.W.*
> *3-4, cloudy, steering S.W. true. Issued half a dipper to each man*
> *and half a biscuit. Hoping for rain showers.*

Sunday dawned cloudy with a slight swell on the sea. The wind had dropped during the night until the boat had lost all way. A light wind sprang up from the north-northwest. The watch trimmed sail hopefully and the boat moved forward once more. Everyone was cheerful over his half biscuit and pittance of water. Their bodies were so dehydrated it was impossible to swallow the hard biscuit without wetting it first. The Mate's eyes narrowed every time he looked inside the breaker. He scanned the sky anxiously for rain clouds, but nowhere in the idly moving mass was one remotely resembling the cloud he sought.

As suddenly as it had come up the breeze dropped. The boat rose and fell on the surface of the sea, her sail hanging slackly from its spar. The sailors swore cheerfully.

All day they drifted aimlessly in this fashion, the sun shining down intensely on them one minute and disappearing behind banks of clouds the next. Talk fell away to nothing save an occasional grunt or stifled exclamation from the wounded men.

Pilcher and Morgan were suffering increasing pain in their wounds. Their lacerated feet had swollen during the night and were swelling more. It was necessary to loosen their bandages. When this had been done, an odor permeated the boat, an odor no man ever forgets once he has smelled it—the horrible stench of gangrene. The Mate examined the wounds intently, but said nothing. He returned to the stern sheets with another weight on his already heavily burdened sense of responsibility.

The men dozed as they drifted, or, sitting up, scanned the empty reaches of the sea. In all that space there was nothing but sky and water to be seen; not a bird, not a patch of seaweed, not even a drifting log.

"Call ye on the Lord all who are in peril of the sea," Widdicombe read from the leaf out of Sparks' book with which he was fashioning a cigarette. The quotation may not be exact, he said later, but the sense was there. "I trust Providence, all right," he told himself, "only let it hurry up." His throat was damnably dry; and every time he looked at poor Pilcher, who was bearing the burning agony of his rotting foot with such gentle fortitude, his Devon nature sensed, if it did not see, a terrifying shadow in the sick man's eyes.

At six o'clock the Mate doled out water. This and the other important event of the day woke the men from their lethargy.

"Sunday treat," he said. "Mutton for dinner today."

"Coo," somebody said.

"Truth," the Mate said, holding up a tin and reading the label. "'Delicious boiled mutton. Thoroughly cool before opening. Slices beautifully.' Will you wait till I chill it or have it now?"

The men watched fascinated while the Mate opened the tin and divided half its contents, six pounds, into seven portions. They took it eagerly, but ate it carefully, making every morsel count. It was more cheering than drink. Soon they were talking away, thirteen to the dozen, their disappointment with the day's progress gone in the acute pleasure of feeling moist animal fat and fiber in their drying mouths and throats.

"Mutton's all right," Widdicombe said, his mouth full, "but give me roast beef, Yorkshire pudding, brown potatoes and plum duff and you can have the rest."

The gunner was all for fish and chips.

"Did you ever eat any of that *bacalhau* at Barcelona—salt codfish and potatoes, fixed up with oil and garlic the way they do? Very good, it is," said Tapscott, reminiscently.

Hawkes did not hold with any foreign food.

"And pickled herrings," Tapscott went on, raptly. "There's nothing I like better. Often I buy a jar of 'em and eat it all myself. I take 'em out by the tail, one by one, like this." He illustrated his method in pantomime, extracting a fish from the jar, holding it over his head and then lowering it into his mouth.

"All we lack now is a pint of bitter," the gunner said.

"Or whiskey and splash," Widdicombe suggested, ironically.

"Beer's best," said Tapscott, seriously. "Spirits are all very well when you want to get drunk; but for regular drinking, beer's the thing. Although I must say I fancy a glass of porter now and again. Odd how they serve whiskey in the States; such tall glasses; and they drown the whiskey!"

The talk fell on drinks and drinking at home and in foreign ports.

"Chap I knew in Newport," Tapscott recounted, "went into a posh bar—one of those places where they don't fill the glasses to the top. He called for beer. When it was given him he called the barmaid back. 'What's this?' he asked. 'The glass of beer you ordered,' she said. 'Call that a glass o' beer?' he said. 'Why don't you fill it up?' ''Tisn't etiquette,' she said. 'Etiquette be blowed!' he said. 'Fill it up.' And she did, although she gave him a look, I can tell you."

Everyone laughed appreciatively.

The sun was sinking in red glory, betokening fair weather to come. The men made ready for the night. The Mate wrote up his log for the day. Had it not been for the disquieting smell of gangrene, which, once in the boat, infected the air, they might have been on a pleasure cruise, so well were they feeling after their hearty meal.

On the back of another of Sparks' time sheets the Mate wrote:

August 25th. Sunday. Crew all well though 2nd. cook and 2nd. W/T wounded feet very painful and starting to swell. Rations half a dipper of water at 6 a.m. and again at 6 p.m. with a little condensed milk. Hoping for rain showers but none around yet. Wind N.N.W. 2, cloudy, slight sea. D/L sail set. Course W.S.W. true. Nothing sighted and becalmed all day long. 6 p.m. opened 6 pound tin of boiled mutton crew ate half which greatly improved their morale which is splendid. No signs of giving up hope. Sun set at 6:35 A.S.T. on leaving ship estimated distance covered 225 miles W. S. W. true.

8. DEATH COMES ABOARD

IN THE morning, Monday, August 26th, their fifth day in the open boat, a bos'n bird appeared to the men of the *Anglo-Saxon*. It planed over them in a leisurely way, wheeled, came back and flew low over them again.

"Mean-looking blighter, he was," Widdicombe said. "Had that look in his eye: 'Just wait. I'll get you yet.'" He stared back at the bird malevolently. "Not me you won't get," he said.

The wind, which had been falling, now dropped away to an occasional fitful gust and the boat drifted or lay becalmed under the burning sun. To men without hats the direct rays were torture. Those who took shelter under the canvas boat cover found themselves in an oven.

They were very thirsty now. Their pores, denied any liquid to evaporate, closed up; their skin scorched and crisped; salivation ceased. The morning half dipper of water, gulped with such eagerness, was like a drop on a blotter.

The Mate gave them the rest of the mutton from the day before. He had wrapped it in moist canvas and stowed it in the locker under the stern seat. It had kept very well but the men had no stomach for it. Without water they had no appetite. Their dehydrated organs and diminished digestive ferments had been unable to assimilate the meal of the night before.

They prayed for squalls and a decent wind.

"We should sight a vessel any time now," the Mate said; and they accepted this as inspired knowledge.

After breakfast, the Mate and the Third dressed the injured men's wounds. Pilcher's mangled foot had swollen to twice its natural size. Without the bandage it was a green and black gangrenous horror. The boat was almost untenable. They gave him the best treatment they could devise with the scant knowledge and means at their disposal. They got his leg over the gunwale. Tapscott bailed salt water over the wound for an hour. The Mate then bound it up with the last linen bandage. Pilcher never flinched, although in exquisite pain. He apologized for giving them so much trouble. "He has guts that one," Widdicombe said to Tapscott. "A proper man if I ever saw one."

Morgan's smashed ankle was swelling badly, too. They gave him the same treatment they had given Sparks.

The bullet hole in the gunlayer's right forearm was still clean. They bathed it with a little of their precious fresh water, saturated it with iodine and bound it up again. The wound in his thigh, however, was not doing at all well. And they were at the end of their medical supplies.

As the sun reached meridian they writhed and twisted on the hot planking of the boat like fish on a griddle. Their mouths and throats were so parched that talking was painful. The able men bailed sea water over the wounded, and when they had them thoroughly doused, went over the side themselves, being careful to keep their faces out of water. Naked, they noted with surprise how much weight they had lost.

"At any rate," the Third said to Tapscott, "you're much better-looking without that fat belly."

Tapscott in his exuberance dived several times and swam under the boat. It did not seem to him that he was any worse off for having got a little sea water in his mouth and nose.

During the long afternoon they dipped themselves again and again, whenever the heat was insupportable. By the time the slanting rays of the setting sun had given them respite they were refreshed and in good spirits. They had their water and condensed milk, half a biscuit, and some of the fat that remained from the tin of mutton.

The Mate, in one of the longest entries in his tragically short log, described the events of the day, seaman fashion.

August 26th. Monday. Bosun bird flew overhead. Sun rose at 6:52 a.m.A.S.T. Becalmed, occasional fitful gusts. Glaring sun rays. Bale out 24 buckets daily. 6 a.m. issued meat rations out from day previous, wrapped up in canvas, little taken, half dipper water per man, little drop of condensed milk, spirits of crew keen, no murmur from wounded men. Hoping to sight vessel soon but praying for squalls and decent wind. During a.m. medical treatment given by 3rd. engineer and myself. W/T operator's left foot which is badly crushed bathed with salt water for an hour and last linen bandage applied, well covered up but swelling badly. 2nd cook's right foot swollen badly, ankle badly strained with bullet wound just above ankle, bathed with salt water and well bandaged. Gunlayer's right forearm washed in fresh water, then iodine applied and bandaged. All day long blinding sun rays and cloudless, becalmed. During afternoon first officer, 3rd. engineer, gunlayer, A.B.'s Widdicombe and Tapscott dipped their bodies in water overside, taking care to keep their faces out of water, result greatly invigorating. Rations still half dipper of water per man at 6 a.m. and 6 p.m., only eat half a biscuit per day, no need for more, and a little condensed milk. The bottled beef kept in canvas still good and the fat is appreciated. Although the W/T is weak, everyone else in good spirits and very cheerful. Keeping two watches, one myself other 3rd. engineer, two A.B.'s, four on and four off. Having no nautical instruments or books on board can only rely on compass and the stars at night. Trusting to make a landfall in vicinity of Leeward Islands, with God's will and British determination, 10:30 p.m. wind freshening from eastward skimming along fine at about 5 knots.

The wind held. Dawn come up partly cloudy. The Mate scanned the skies for the least sign of rain. There was nothing. He doled out the morning ration of water as if each drop was his own blood. No one wanted food. Nothing was said; no one complained; but it was obvious that the tempo of life in the boat was slowing down.

Using half a tin of Sparks' tobacco and leaves from his book of Biblical quotations for papers, the Mate managed a cigarette for each man, then noted in the log: "Only eight matches left so this luxury will soon be stopped."

They made good progress during the day. Whenever they spoke, which was seldom, they heard the changed notes of their voices distorted by thirst. Cracked and swollen lips, tightened skin and salient cheek bones gave them new expressions. They noticed that they were not so sure of their footing as before.

That evening, to buck up morale the Mate held a lottery. Lotteries and pools are dear to the British seamen. Every fo'castle has them: football pools, sweepstakes, anything that offers the possibility of getting much for little. Seven days were chosen—September 9th to September 15th—as those upon which they would be picked up by a ship or make a landfall. These were listed on a sheet with a space next the date for the name of the man who drew it in the lottery. The men's names were then written on slips of paper, scrambled in Sparks' cap, and drawn by the cook. The losers were bound by the lottery to buy the winner all the drinks he could consume.

The lottery was a great success. They were vociferous in cracked and raucous voices over the dates they had drawn. Sparks was convinced that he would be the winner. He worked this out by some private system of numerology. They settled down for the night, still arguing the matter. The mere act of holding a lottery based on their rescue seemed, somehow to assure the fact.

During the night the boat did a steady four knots on the port tack heading S.W. true. The sun, the Mate noted, had set at 6:42.

The trade wind held all the next day. In the morning a bos'n bird and a common gull flew over them. "There's that bloody bird again," Widdicombe said, shaking his fist at it. "What's he want hanging about like this?" The men laughed. But Widdicombe was serious. "He had mean eyes," he said. "It made me fair narked."

The sun beat down tropically. The Mate, the Third, Tapscott and Widdicombe dipped their bodies overside again, holding on to the life lines that festooned the side of the boat. Their bodies took up the water through their pores leaving their skin white with salt. Saliva returned to their mouths. They all felt better.

The reek of gangrene was terrible now. Penny's torn hip was going the way of Pilcher's foot. No matter how brisk the breeze, it seemed impossible to get that devastating stench out of their nostrils. Sparks was apologetic. It was the only sign of suffering he allowed himself. Morgan's wound was gangrening, too. Everyone assured Sparks that it was nothing that could be helped, but on awakening to it, after the unconsciousness of sleep, their stomachs turned over.

In the morning Sparks' foot "went dead." He no longer felt pain in it. He no longer felt anything there. It was surcease of a sort but bought at the expense of his whole body. He was failing and they caught in his eyes the expression of a man who is looking beyond life.

The wind was strong and the sea boisterous. They bowled along handily, making fine time and shipping buckets of water. No one cared about the water. They were soaking wet, yet all they talked of was liquids. They talked of peaches, pears, oranges, the juice of pineapples. In the end, they talked of beer: light beer, dark beer, beer in glasses, mugs and tankards; English, Danish, French and German beer; beer foaming from inexhaustible taps. Some of this wistful preoccupation insinuated itself into the Mate's dry and laconic log. He wrote:

> *Gig running free on port tack heading S.W. true. High hopes of picking up ship or making landfall shortly. We are all putting our trust in God's hands. Everyone well except a weakness in legs and, of course, great loss in weight. Do not feel particularly hungry but suffer from parched throat owing to low water ration. Pity we have no lime juice or tins of fruit, which would ease matters considerably, but no one is complaining.*

They made ready for a wet night cheerfully. This they told themselves, in voices croaking with thirst, was the last lap.

In the morning the wind dropped and the swell lessened. After the first bite no one cared to go on with his quarter of a ship's biscuit. It was impossible to swallow. The half dipper of water gave them a few moments' release from the grip at their throats; then it was gone, a splatter of rain in the desert of their desiccated tissues.

Pilcher lay very quietly now under the shelter of the boat cover. As the sun climbed the sky and the temperature mounted and the men bailed water over one another. Morgan, the cook, seemed better; he could move his stiffened leg. Penny seemed better, too; so much so he took a short trick at the tiller.

Everyone remarked that they had stopped sweating, even at noon. The dryness of their throats crawled up their tongues, which, thick and discolored, filled their mouths like a gag of hot felt. They grinned at each other now and then as if sharing a painful, sardonic joke.

In the evening, the wind fell away completely. The boat pitched, tossed and drifted on the swell. It was hard to rest, much less to sleep, thrown about on a narrow seat. They were awake until late at night.

Just as, fatigued to the point of sleep, some of them achieved an uneasy doze, Pilcher's voice rose from the bow in a long and plangent wail. An inhuman quality in it, a severance from all direction of the intellect, brought them awake with a start.

"What is it, Sparks?" the Mate asked.

There was no answer.

The Mate went forward to him. He was lying face upward, staring unseeingly into the sky.

"What's the matter?" the Mate repeated.

The glazed eyes showed no flicker of recognition. A voice, a detached caricature of Pilcher's, apostrophized an unseen, abstract personage in bitter, obscene invective. The voice, matter and manner were utterly unlike the normal gentle Sparks! Then he laughed—hysterical bursts of unmotivated laughter, which stopped as abruptly and unreasonably as they had started.

"Off his head," the Mate said, "and that's a fact."

Sparks was singing now, a street ballad of the most scabrous nature, a song they would not have thought him capable of. He sang it to the end, then started again. He sang it over and over.

"For God's sake, stop him!" Morgan, who lay next him, begged the Mate.

The Mate tried again to quiet the delirious operator, but to no use. Sparks, insulated by hysteria, gave no sign of hearing anything. All they could do was wait uneasily for the seizure to wear itself out.

After a bit Sparks subsided into low moans and a running mutter of talk. The men settled themselves again. They could not sleep, no matter how they twisted and turned; expectancy of what they did not want to hear kept them tense. It came very soon, heralded by that long-drawn, rising, animal cry—singing, invective, bursts of maniacal laughter.

Toward the morning Sparks drifted off into sleep or semi-coma. The Mate wrote up his log:

> *Moderate N.E. trades and swell; course W.S.W. true. Rationed half a dipper of water at 6 a.m. and again at 6 p.m. Now 1/4 biscuit per man. Hardly touched now owing slim issue of water, small issue thin condensed milk. Crew's spirits cheerful but W/T operator getting weaker, during evening becoming becalmed W/T operator delirious. Kept everyone awake at night with moans.*

The next day the Mate wrote:

> *Becalmed, partly cloudy, nothing sighted whatsoever. Have not had one speck of rain but living in hopes. 6:15 a.m. water issue half a dipper also at 6:30 p.m. Opened our second tin boiled mutton (six pounds) have one left, also five tins condensed milk and 3/4 case hard biscuits. Water half gone. Nine days in boat.*

At sun-up the next morning the Mate called the able men to him. "We've got to do something about Sparks's foot," he said.

All of the previous day Sparks had alternated between delirium and comatose sleep. He had been off his head most of the night and was now exhausted but lucid.

"What can we do?" they asked.

"Amputate it."

"With what?" Tapscott asked.

"The axe. If we don't, he's going to die."

Tapscott was shocked. The axe was rusty, dirty and dull. They had no antiseptic. He was certain, too—but he did not mention this to the others—that Sparks was going to die anyway. Why torture him with a clumsy operation that would in all likelihood end in him bleeding to death?

The men looked uncertainly at one another.

"I know it's taking a long chance," the Mate said, "but that foot is poisoning him. It will have to come off."

Hawkes and Widdicombe agreed that the Mate was right, but Tapscott still demurred.

"Very well," said the Mate, "we'll put it up to Sparks himself."

They went forward to Pilcher, who lay in the bow-sheets, weak but uncomplaining.

"Sparks, old chap," the Mate said, "your foot is in bad shape."

"I know it," Sparks said, feebly.

"We think it will have to come off. The sooner the better. Do you want us to do it?"

"Yes. Please. Anything," Pilcher said, his face contorted with pain.

The Mate fetched the axe. They removed the boat cover from Pilcher. Widdicombe and Hawkes stood by to hold him. But when it come to the actual business of lopping off Sparks' foot with the axe, even the resolute Mate quailed. "I can't do it," he said. "He'll just have to take the chance."

Everyone breathed a sigh of relief.

The Mate rearranged the boat cover over Pilcher so as to keep the sun off his face. "Carry on, old boy," he said. "We're not going to do it now. We're certain to be picked up soon and a proper doctor will make it right for you."

Pilcher smiled weakly and closed his eyes.

Saturday night was grim and miserable. They were so thirsty they could not sleep. In the morning the Mate wrote in his log:

During Saturday night crew felt very thirsty; boiled mutton could not be digested and some felt sick. Doubled water ration that night.

This was a triumph of understatement. When the Mate used the word "sick" he did not mean ill, as Americans do, but, literally, nauseated. Nor did he say that of the "some" who were sick he was the sickest. Nausea and cramps seized him early in the night, causing him to retch agonizedly. Had the others not been so tormented themselves, they would have been more concerned.

When the morning dawned, they saw to their consternation that he, the symbol of discipline and fountainhead of knowledge, had suffered some sort of internal collapse. His face was livid and lined with pain. All of his strength seemed to have gone from him. His abraded fingers were suppurating badly, and his flesh, even where burned by the sun, had a lifeless, claylike appearance.

Pilcher, too, was very low. He was so weak he could hardly speak. He was lucid, though. When they took him his morning ration of water he turned his head from the dipper and told them to give it to someone who needed it more than he.

They went about the business of the boat in a vague and silent fashion. The sun was already hot enough to be uncomfortable. It reflected back from the sea, giving them a taste of the burning misery to come.

At eight o'clock, Morgan, from his place next to Pilcher in the bow-sheets said, suddenly: "I say, I think Sparks has gone."

The Mate, the Third, Tapscott and Widdicombe went forward. Morgan had spoken the truth. Sparks had, indeed, gone, as silently and unobtrusively as he had done everything in life. They looked at one another incredulously. So soon! It couldn't be possible. But when the looked at Sparks' fallen jaw and saw the subtle changes that had already taken place in the contours of his face, they knew that it could not be otherwise. They stood impotently by, overwhelmed by the awful finality of death.

In curt, low orders the Mate arranged all that was left to do. Tapscott and the Third lifted the body over the gunwale and lowered it gently into the sea. They had nothing to wrap it in and nothing with which to weigh it.

The wind was south-southwest; the boat was making several knots. The body drifted away on the swell, off into the immensity of the Atlantic. They watched it until they could see it no more.

To Tapscott it seemed a surpassing indecency that a man should be buried so. He was no stranger to death, but it was always death cloaked in the decent habiliments of civil or naval ceremony. It seemed to him, too, that with Pilcher's going something of his own life, of all their lives, had gone. He dropped listlessly down on a thwart.

In the log the Mate wrote:

W/T operator passed peacefully away. Committed his body to the deep with silent prayer.

Very little was said in the boat the rest of that day.

9. ORDEAL BY THIRST

WHEN THE sun came up the next morning, their twelfth in the open boat, there was no expectant stir, no sense of a new day. Pilcher's death was heavy upon them and the Mate's condition gave them new cause for alarm. He could scarcely crawl to the breaker to issue the morning half dipper of water. His face was ghastly, his will and vitality almost gone.

Several of them refused the ration of dry ship's biscuit. Those who took it gave up trying to eat; they were unable to chew.

Penny, the gunner, lay quiet in the bow. He was visibly much weaker. Morgan, who had lain beside him, almost as quietly, since the ordeal by thirst began, now chattered and sang. There was this difference though: formerly he would overwhelm anyone who would listen with his garrulousness, now he talked to himself. He returned to his favorite song, with the refrain that "not one in a million would ever complain," and sang it as a hymn of lamentation. He sang it to the end and then took up the first line again, over and over, until the other men, somber and suffering, yelled to him to keep still. He was drinking salt water, too. They suspected that he drank more than they knew—at night.

Tapscott, also, drank salt water. Whenever his thirst became intolerable he eased his rasped throat with a can of it scooped from the sea. It helped for a moment but did not satisfy him. He could not see that he suffered any ill effect from it except excessive purgation.

Widdicombe, too, seemed bordering on hysteria, alternately violently optimistic, confident that they would come through all right in the end, or sunk in apathetic pessimism. He suffered more than the others from the heat. He attributed this to a sunstroke he had experienced on a voyage through the Arabian Sea. Frequently he would be overcome while taking his turn at the tiller and would have to get Tapscott to relieve him until the faintness had passed.

Tapscott, engrossed in his own misery, brooded over this. He doubted Widdicombe's peculiar susceptibility as he doubted many of Widdicombe's stories. He had never liked Widdicombe and he felt that his watch mate was exploiting him now, trading on his good nature to get out of onerous duty. This growing resentment blazed forth in open quarrel that morning, which might have ended tragically had the Third not intervened. Widdicombe had called Tapscott to relieve him of the tiller, saying that he was about to faint. Tapscott, having had enough of this, refused. Hot words followed, unprintable insults were exchanged, in which all their natural antipathy, exacerbated by the misery of their situation, came into the open. Widdicombe leaped at Tapscott. Tapscott reached for the Mates' axe. The Third threw his arms about Tapscott and ordered Widdicombe to give over. Discipline, obviously weakening, was restored for the time.

Discipline now was sustained only by a symbol, the Mate. So long as he lived and retained his reason he held command. But as the sun rose higher and the heat increased, violent nausea and spasms of pain racked him. He lay in the bottom of the boat, retching horribly. After one of these spells he would lie exhausted, in a state of semi-coma. His arms were a mass of blisters and scales. In spite of all this, he took a turn at the tiller whenever he could.

To Morgan, also, they gave a trick at the rudder. It seemed to allay his growing dementia, and weak as they now were, everyone had to help. But Morgan gave them more trouble than aid. He seemed incapable of grasping the first principles of sailing a boat. He yawed and blundered, shipping water and nearly capsizing them several times. This always happened, it seemed, the moment the watch from the exposed stern had got to sleep under the protection of the canvas boat cover.

They made little progress that day. No one had the energy to dip himself overside. They simply lay and suffered, protecting themselves from the worst of the sun with the boat cover.

That evening the Mate made the last entry he was able to write in the log. He reported their condition with his habitual understatement. As ill and despairing as he was he remained the officer. He included a suggestion for bettering life-boat equipment based upon his all too actual experience. In a hand that could just trace the letters he wrote:

> *Sept. 2nd. Monday. 6:15 a.m. issued half a dipper of water per man and same in evening with a little condensed milk diluted with it. Crew now feeling rather low, unable to masticate hard biscuit owing to low ration of water.*
>
> Suggestion for life-boat stocks. *At the very least two breakers of water for each boat, tins of fruit such as peaches, apricots, pears, fruit juices and lime juices, baked beans, etc. Our stores consisted of:—*

One tank filled with dry biscuit.
11 tins condensed milk
  3 tins each 6 pounds boiled mutton.
One breaker of water, half filled.

These were the last words of any kind the Mate ever wrote. He was ill all during the night and so weak in the morning he could not get to his feet. They made a bed for him in the thwarts, using boards and life-belts. He was too ill now to command.

The traditional controversy between deck and engine-room flared up. The Third Engineer as an officer automatically took over command. Widdicombe objected violently. The deck was senior to the engine-room, and what did the Third know about sailing a boat, he wanted to know. The Third rested on his rank; no matter which branch of the merchant service was senior—a question he saw no reason to debate—he was senior to Widdicombe, he pointed out.

"All right," said Widdicombe in a temper, "sail the bloody boat yourself then."

The argument ended in a compromise: Hawkes would deal the rations and keep the log; Widdicombe would direct the sailing of the boat.

A fair breeze had sprung up from the east-southeast. Whatever was in store for them, they must keep going west. It was their only hope. They trimmed sail and kept the boat on her course.

When the Third went to the water breaker Widdicombe proposed issuing a whole dipperful instead of the usual ration. Tapscott objected; he was as thirsty as anyone but he felt they should maintain the ration the Mate had decided upon up to the very end. And that would be all too soon, they knew; the water was very near the bottom of the breaker now.

The Third hesitated. The Mate was too ill to intervene. Penny and Morgan were nullities so far as making decisions was concerned;

Penny was nearly as weak as the Mate and Morgan had to be handled like a feeble-minded child.

"The water won't last much longer anyway," Widdicombe insisted, "so why not have a decent drink now?"

In the end Hawkes and Tapscott gave in. There was that in Widdicombe's voice and manner which caused them to fear that he would attempt to take the water by force. They did not want a fight to complete their distress. A fight was the last thing in the world they wanted at that moment.

That day they made better time than on the day before. They took their turns at the tiller, bailed the boat and sought shelter from the sun under the boat cover, trying not to think of the thirst that was consuming them.

They were dull with apprehension, but, whatever their thoughts were, they did not express them. Each man was wholly preoccupied with his chief concern, his own life. That is, all but Morgan, who kept up a babble of senseless talk and singing until one of them, driven into a passion of irritation, would silence him temporarily with a curse.

Tapscott thought of nothing in particular; he was sunk into a heat-drenched stupor, a sort of anesthesia. He was not despondent, though. Things were pretty bad, he realized, but they need not inevitably end in disaster. He was nineteen years old, and life, even in such circumstances as these, was essentially a hopeful affair.

Widdicombe, mercurial in his calmest moments, alternated between energetic optimism and angry despair. This he relieved at times by cursing, long and fervently, an abstract fate that could not be reached with his fists and feet.

The older men, one poisoned with gangrenous wounds, the other, ravaged by some internal disorder in addition to the thirst and starvation they were all suffering, said nothing. Neither could have had much hope, unless that of a miraculous landfall or rescue ship, but neither of them would admit it. Both must have known that rescue for them would be too late now.

The Third wrote up the log:

Sept 3rd. Tuesday. One dipper of water per man at 7 a.m. again in evening. First Mate who wrote this diary up to this point going fast. Good breezes from E.S.E.

The night was chill and wet. Their teeth chattered as they huddled together for warmth. The Mate kept them awake with the violence of his vomiting, the cook with hysterical ramblings and complaint. Toward morning the cook became quieter.

The sun rose on a calmer sea. The wind fell off and the boat made slow progress under a sky that promised no escape from another day of unbearable heat and thirst. They had the morning ration of water. It was plain that after the next drink there would be no more. They were at the very end of their tether.

The noon sun reduced them to such an agony of thirst they voted to drink the last of the water then and there. It was measured out, the three able men jealously watching that an exact division was made.

Tapscott sat on the starboard seat. Widdicombe and the Third were at the breaker. Morgan was lying in the bow-sheets and the Mate on his bed of boards amidships. Penny had just taken the tiller. He said nothing, but there was nothing unusual in that. Normally taciturn, Penny had practically quit speech in the last few days.

The boat yawed suddenly. Tapscott turned to see what the helmsman was up to. But there was no helmsman to be seen. Where Penny had sat there was an empty seat and the rudder handle swinging purposelessly. Tapscott sprang to his feet and searched the sea. Then he saw Penny. He was floating away rapidly, face downward his arms outstretched before him. "Like doing the deadman's float,"

Tapscott said. He was making no attempt to swim. He had not gone over for that.

Even if they had been able to bring the boat about in time—which was impossible—it is doubtful if anyone would have moved to go after the gunner. He was doing what he deemed best. Unwritten law gave a man in these circumstances, provided he was or appeared to be in his right mind, the inalienable right to choose his own way out of his suffering. The gunner had "gone over the side."

The Third seized the tiller and put the boat back on its course. They discussed the manner of Penny's going. Unmentioned, it had been in the minds of all of them at one time or another.

"I never thought he'd do it," Tapscott said.

"We may all have to," the Mate said from his bed.

"That's better than going on to the very end," the Third said. "But *I* couldn't do it. Someone would have to knock me out first. I'm afraid of the water."

"Me, too," Tapscott said.

Widdicombe's eyes were rolling in his head. "Not me," he said. "I want to live."

Morgan said something different in the middle of his stream of chatter. But no one heard him. They were not listening to him.

It was hard to take in, but, they had to admit, this very likely *was* the end. It confronted them suddenly with a horrible actuality. There was nothing more for them, saving a miracle, than prolonged torture, madness and inevitable death. They had known that it was a possibility but had kept it so buried in their minds, resolutely determined not to admit it, it seemed a new and unfair hardship considering what they had already endured.

Better end it now and spare themselves further suffering. That would be the sensible course, they agreed. But a physical lassitude weighed down their bodies and paralyzed their wills. No one wanted the initiative in so final a move. In the end they did nothing but mechanically sail the boat, and there was no more talk of going over the side.

The Third even made an entry in the log. Something of his certainty that this was the last one is apparent in it. He had not read the Mate's earlier entries, so he did not know that the facts of the sinking of the *Anglo-Saxon* had already been set down. They were slipping out of life rapidly, thanks to the inhumanity of their foe. He must leave some record of the inhuman thing that had been done!

He wrote:

> *September 4th. Everybody very much weaker. The Mate is going fast now. 1:30 p.m. today Penny very much weaker slipped overboard. From 10 p.m. tonight 14 days out. Tried to make Leeward Islands or Porto Rico, Hayti, but the German raider given none the right to take a sextant, chronometer, extra water, tin or bottled fruit. No rum or brandy for wounded crew. Evidently intended to smash all life-boat gear to kill all inquiry, but we got off in small gig, seven of us by wind somewhere in the vicinity of the Leeward Islands.*

It was his farewell message, made the more bitter by his belief that they were near their objective. Many hundred sun-struck sea miles lay between them and the Leeward Islands.

Night brought escape from the heat, at least. They sprawled or lay in misery, all power gone from their limbs. When they moved to relieve one another at the tiller the physical action lagged appreciably behind the act of will. It seemed too great an effort to get themselves from the bow to the stern of the boat.

The wind was slight and fitful. The boat drifted or sailed listlessly. At times it seemed to float stationary, its only motion a slight heaving with the swell.

The Mate was scarcely breathing. Morgan had quieted down. There was no sound just before dawn, save the sighs of the sleeping men and the murmur of the sea.

Morgan sat up suddenly, pushed away the canvas that was muffling him, stared into the void and said peremptorily: "I want my mother."

10. SAILOR'S LEAVE

I

DAY DAWNED to the five men aboard the *Anglo-Saxon*—their thirteenth in the open boat—as the morning of execution to a condemned man.

The sun came up from the sea; the breeze freshened; the boat picked up speed. But the unkempt, hollow-eyed, thirst-tortured creatures in it hardly stirred.

From habit they edged toward the water breaker. Then, remembering, they sat down again. They were heavy with apprehension. Each regarded the other warily, awaiting the gesture or word they all knew would come.

As if to put the seal of finality on disaster, the rudder, which lacked a lower pintle when they left the ship, was carried away by a heavy swell. The Mate was steering at the time. He watched it disappear as if it were his last hope for life, dropped the useless tiller, went to his bed of life-belts and boards, and lay down with closed eyes.

Tapscott and Widdicombe got out the steering oar and shipped it in place of the lost rudder. The Third, who had been watching the Mate narrowly, stretched himself out beside him. The two lay this way for a long time, while the sun, mounting higher, burned into their eyelids and whipped up the demon inside, which was relentlessly squeezing the juice of life from them.

They sailed for long hours this way, hearing nothing, seeing nothing. Then the Mate opened his eyes, raised himself on his elbow and said from swollen and discolored lips, "I'm going over. Who's coming with me?"

"No, no! Don't! You can't! Don't leave me! You won't, will you?" Morgan cried from the bowsheets.

"Shut up!" Widdicombe ordered him, menacing him with a gesture.

Morgan was still.

Tapscott, Widdicombe and the Third stared at one another, each waiting for the other to speak.

"I'll go," the Third said, finally; "only you'll have to help me, you know."

The Mate nodded assent. He turned his eyes to Morgan.

"No, no, no!" Morgan cried. "I can't. I can't. I don't want to die."

The Mate turned next to Tapscott. Tapscott thought a minute before answering. "No," he said. He felt that he must explain. "I mean to say," he added, "it isn't like I was dying; and you can't tell; we may be picked up yet."

The Mate turned to Widdicombe. Widdicombe shook his head violently. "No fear," he said, showing the whites of his eyes like a nervous horse.

The Mate lay back with eyes closed.

"That settles that," said the Third. "I might as well have some sleep myself before we go." He lay down beside the mate again.

The dread of what they must see overwhelmed the other three. Morgan lay back in the bow-sheets staring at the self-condemned men. It was the formal end; those in command were laying down their arms.

"Maybe," Tapscott thought, "they'll change their minds." He could not imagine anyone making such a dreadful decision and then going calmly to sleep.

Neither Tapscott nor Widdicombe would have dreamed of remonstrating or trying to interfere. Not only were the two officers senior to them and entitled to make decisions without question, but they had decided the most private question in life. Interference would have been presumptuousness of the most outrageous character. Moreover, they were too dazed and miserable themselves to formulate more than their own desire to hold on until the last. Tapscott did not even think that far; blind instinct had spoken for him, an instinct he had never thought to question.

There was something awesome in this vigil. They sailed for an hour or more in this fashion.

Somewhere near ten o'clock Hawkes sat up and said: "Ready?"

The Mate opened his eyes and then got to his feet with surprising speed and sureness, considering how weak he had been. He picked up the axe and placed it on a thwart near the port gunwale.

"Just a minute," Hawkes said, almost gaily. "I'm going to have something to eat and drink." He dipped a can of water from the sea and gulped it down greedily. He filled the can again and drank that off. Then he softened a biscuit in sea water and ate it.

The Mate drew off his signet ring and handed it to Widdicombe. "Give it—my mother—if you get through," he gasped.

They shook hands all around.

It was then that Hawkes had a moment of bitterness. "To think," he said, "that I put in four years of training—to come to this."

The Mate took off his coat. Hawkes removed his, too.

"Give it to me," Widdicombe said.

"No," the Third said, "I can't. I promised it to Bob if anything happened to me."

"Then give me your trousers," Widdicombe said. "You won't need them."

"Can't do that either," the Third said, grinning through cracked and blistered lips; "I might meet a mermaid where I'm going."

"Tapscott's eyes were blinded with unexpected tears when the Mate took his hand.

"Keep going west," the Mate said, scarcely able to force the words through his stiffened lips. His voice fell off into a throaty croak; he gestured loosely with his left hand and struggled to achieve what he wanted to say. "No more south."

The Mate and the Third then stood up in the thwarts near the port gunwale. They shook hands. Tapscott turned his head away and held his breath. He heard a crunching thud, a great splash, and, when he dared look again, the Mate and the Third were floating yards away, clasped, apparently, in each other's arms.

The Third's hair, the lightest of yellows normally, had bleached to white in the boat. Long and untrimmed, it floated out on the sea like a patch of bright sea-growth, a brilliant note in the monotone of blue water. The men in the boat could see it for a long time. Getting smaller and smaller, they found and lost it in the swell until it, too, became a part of the heaving whole.

"We ought to pray," Morgan said, with surprising clarity and sense.

"What shall we say?" they asked.

They were at a loss for a minute and then decided upon the Lord's Prayer.

"Our Father Who art in Heaven," they prayed, standing unsteadily in the heaving boat, Widdicombe clutching the steering oar. They stumbled through to the end.

Tapscott was ashamed to discover that he had forgotten part of the prayer. He had not forgotten the bright pattern of Hawkes' hair upon the sea, though. It still comes back to him at night. He fears it will come back to him nights as long as he lives.

II

THE PASSING of the Mate and the Third Engineer had a curious effect upon Widdicombe. It vitalized him into hope and action. He took to himself command.

Morgan and Tapscott were sunk in despair. Widdicombe, on the contrary, was full of energy. He trimmed sail, set the course and rallied the others to new effort.

In his role as commander he took charge of the log and made an entry. It followed the last notation of Hawkes. He wrote:

> *September 23rd. Chief Mate and Third Engineer go over side. No water.*

They had nothing to maintain life—neither food nor water—but Widdicombe was sure that somehow, perhaps miraculously, they would come through.

Tapscott, wretched, grieving and sorrowful, was, at bottom, taking it all in his stride, as he had taken everything in his short life. Come fair, come foul, he would carry on, neither daunted by adversity nor made foolish by success. He clung to life tenaciously, but without parade. If die he must, he would do it, calmly, in the same way that he lived. Deep within him, too, was an obstinate sense of justice and a capacity for disciplined enmity, once he was convinced that he had been wronged, as unshakable and enduring as his instinct for life.

Morgan, whose self-control had never been strong, was so shaken by what he had been through, he now abandoned himself completely to terror. They could bully or cajole him into silence for a few minutes or some show of discipline, but, left to himself any length of time, he slipped off into hysteria or bursts of insane activity.

Morgan's disability was a serious disadvantage. The were so weak that an hour at the steering oar was about all one man could manage at a time.

They moved now like figures in a slow-motion film. They had to rest continuously to husband what little strength they had left. They divided the day into hour watches, which they kept more or less accurately, although they had to shorten or lengthen them often according to their physical state.

The mere thought of food gave Tapscott a painful contraction of the stomach, which seized him like a cramp. He would have to lie down while suffering it and wait until it had passed before he could do a thing.

Widdicombe suffered more and more from the sun. It gave him fits of vertigo that rendered him useless for whatever he was doing at the time.

They tried Morgan on the steering oar and it seemed to steady him for a time. But, always, in the end, they had to snatch it away from him to avoid disaster. He could not stay on the wind or learn the rudiments of handling the boat in the swell. They took bucketfuls of water which had to be laboriously bailed out. And they could scarcely stand on their legs.

That night they put out the sea-anchor and lay to. It was impossible in their weakened state to stand night watches. Huddled under the boat cover they courted sleep.

Morgan was fairly quiet until midnight; then delirium seized him again. He moaned, raved, sang and went through his whole ghastly repertory. The seizures were of longer duration now. The fissure in his reasoning widening.

The second day after the Mate and the Third went over was very like the first, save that the breeze lessened and the heat increased.

They bailed sea water over each other and dipped their heads over the side when the sun was at its worst.

Tapscott noticed impersonally, as if it was not his body he was considering, that his skin was cracking and scaling, and that he was covered with boil-like eruptions. The piece of shrapnel in his left palm was working to the surface. It made a painful lump there which prevented him from grasping anything firmly. As consumed as he was by his thirst, he drank no more sea water. The Third's last actions before going over made him somehow chary of that.

Morgan, on the other hand, drank sea water in greater quantities. It did no good to warn him not to or to stop him in the act. At night he could dip it up when he chose.

That night they lay hove to again, but got very little sleep. Morgan kept them awake with his noise and lamentations. The next day he was worse. They put him in the bow-sheet under the boat cover, wedged in well with life-belts, and ordered him to lie still. Tapscott had no sooner made his way aft again than Morgan was out of his shelter and working his way aft. Or, worse, he would pull himself up on the gunwale and try to walk, at imminent peril of falling overboard.

The breeze was lighter and the humidity intense. Widdicombe sat a great deal of the time with his head in his hands. His burst of optimism and energy had departed as suddenly as it had arrived. He would shut out Morgan's ravings with the palms of his hands, or bear them until his frayed nerves recoiled. Then he would stagger up and rave and curse like a madman himself.

In the heat of the day, while staring at nothing, Widdicombe got up suddenly, went to the water breaker, took the keg from its cradle and hurled it into the sea.

"That's a damn silly thing to do," Tapscott said to him. "What did you want to do that for?"

"Why is it sitting there with nothing in it?" Widdicombe demanded furiously.

"Now what will we put the water in when it rains?" Tapscott asked.

"We aren't going to get any water. It's never going to rain. What do I care, anyway?" Widdicombe shrieked.

Tapscott mentally shrugged his shoulders. He wondered if Widdicombe, too, were going completely off his head.

They lay to that night and tried to get some sleep. The second cook was in and out of the bow-sheets all the time. When not raving he sank into coma and at such moments they dozed.

The next day was like the one before. Widdicombe was now sunk in deepest dejection. Morgan laughed, cried, shouted and sang, practically continuously. He varied this with demands for his mother. This, particularly, roused Widdicombe to fury.

"Shut up!" he yelled at Morgan, unable to support more. "Do you think *you're* the only one that wants his mother?"

The insane man was quiet for several minutes. He gave no sign of understanding a word of what had been said to him, but something in the tone of Widdicombe's voice penetrated to that distant spot to which his intelligence had withdrawn.

In the afternoon Morgan seemed to be clearing up mentally. He was quiet and spoke almost normally. Encouraged, Tapscott and Widdicombe put him at the steering oar and tried to get some of the sleep they had lost the night before. They had just dozed off when the boat swung wildly and took a big sea, drenching Widdicombe to the skin. Widdicombe leaped up. Morgan was on his feet, too, the boat left to the vagaries of the swell. Widdicombe threw himself on Morgan. In the struggle that followed the cook went overboard. Tapscott, always a heavy sleeper, awoke in time to see the cook disappear. Flinging himself over the gunwale he seized him by the hair, and, after a desperate effort, managed to get him back into the boat.

Widdicombe flung himself down in the bottom of the boat and gave himself to a fit of hysteria nearly as wild as the cook's.

Morgan's dementia rose as the day wore on. It mounted to such a pitch of frenzy that Tapscott, normally imperturbable, thought that he, too, would go off his head if the cook did not quiet down and let him sleep. The stream of babbling, shouting, crying and singing flowed on endlessly until every nerve in his body was crawling.

Widdicombe tried to shout the cook into silence, but it was too late for that now. Exhausted by his effort, Widdicombe lay in the bottom of the boat, his breath coming in great gulps, his hands working.

The cook paused for a moment, took a breath and began all over again. With a despairing shriek Widdicombe leaped to his feet, picked up the axe and threw it blindly in the cook's direction. It went wide of the mark and dropped into the sea.

Tapscott, too weak and done down himself to do more than grunt a protest, saw the axe go with regret. He had counted on it for cutting a hole in one of the air-tight tanks, if and when they had a rain. The tanks were all that they had now that would serve to hold water in any amount.

They drifted and sailed aimlessly until sun-down and then went through the familiar and weary ritual of lowering the sail, putting out the sea-anchor, and lying to. They pulled the boat cover over them and longed for sleep—anything to get away from the slow fire that was consuming them inwardly. But Morgan's dementia would not let them rest. What was torture by day became nightmare at night. The peak came toward early morning; then he subsided into coma, broken now and then by muttering and groaning.

The sun rose in a sky bright and clear. With scorched and blood-shot eyes they searched the heavens for signs of rain. The air was heavier and more humid than it had been, but there were only a few thin high clouds and a steady breeze. With leaden hands they got in the sea-anchor and set sail again west, resigning themselves to another day of suffering.

Morgan lay in the bow quietly, his eyes closed. Tapscott nodded at the steering oar; Widdicombe was stretched out on the port seat, the side that shipped the least water. They would go on this way until midday when the sun, they knew, would be unendurable and they would have to bail water over one another.

Morgan pushed away the boat cover and got up. His expression was normal and his voice firm, clear and without the detached quality of insanity.

"I think," he said, as casually as if they had all been at home in a Newport house, "I'll go down the street for a drink." He climbed up on the seat, walked aft rapidly, and before they could rouse themselves, or even realize what was afoot, stepped over the side. He went down like a shot. When his body reappeared it was being carried away by the swell. He made no more movement, no outcry. They stood staring stupidly after him. Then they sat down and stared at each other. Of the seven men of the *Anglo-Saxon* they were all that was left.

Widdicombe was first to rouse himself. Some sense of his duty as keeper of the log seemed to stir him. He fumbled in Sparks' attaché case for the sheets upon which the log was kept. In a weak and shaking hand he wrote:

September 9th. 2nd cook goes mad; dies. Only two of us left.

11. REPRIEVE

I

AT THE time of the second cook's going neither Tapscott nor Widdicombe could say honestly that they regretted it; they felt that he was better off. They felt little of anything except the weakness that benumbed them, the violent pains and cramps that racked them and the slow, relentless pressure of their drying bodies. The sudden removal of the psychological torture of the cook's raving was, if anything, a relief.

They sailed on, the sun climbing the heavens, until the straightening rays drove them to the shelter of the boat cover. They lay there suffering, debating whether they had not better go over the side themselves.

Widdicombe was for holding on as long as possible. Tapscott, by nature co-operative and agreeable, said he would do whatever Widdicombe did.

At high noon their thirst was so terrible they were driven to drinking urine. They feared the effects of sea water, but Tapscott, when he could stand the torture no longer, took a little to allay for a minute the burning and aching of his closing throat.

The sea water made Tapscott sick. He was shaken with a paroxysm of vomiting, after which he lay quietly for a long time. As intelligence flickered up in him again he wondered whether he had best go over now, while he still had the strength to do it. A few seconds' struggle in the cool, wet sea, a brief act of will, and then oblivion. Surely, it would be much better that way.

Cramping pains tore at Widdicombe's entrails, stretching him stiff in the bottom of the boat. He rolled about in agony, clutching at his belly and bursting into bellows of insane rage and hysterical imprecation.

The sun crossed the meridian and moved snaillike down the sky. As the heat diminished their suffering lightened. They lay in grateful stupor—how long they had no idea. When the sun finally set and the welcome darkness lowered they were just able to get the sea-anchor over and the boat made ready for the night. They fell back into a state of sleep and suffering. But such sleep as they achieved—if it could be called sleep—gave them no refreshment. When the sun rose the next morning they knew it was day—and little more.

The wind dropped. The boat lost all way. It wallowed gently on an oily sea under a hot and humid sky. The tempo of the elements slowed down to the faint pulse of life in the boat.

"Oh, God damn it all," Tapscott said, with a kind of cosmic petulance, "I'm going over. Are you with me?"

Widdicombe nodded faintly.

Tapscott crawled to Sparks' attaché case and got out pencil and paper. Laboriously he scrawled a note to his mother. He said that there was nothing left to hope for, good-bye, and that he sent all his love. He put the note back into the case with the log and other records. He was sure the boat would be picked up eventually.

"Come on, then," he said, lowering himself over the side. Widdicombe followed. But, as Widdicombe's body slid into the water, he suffered a violent revulsion. He pulled himself up again on the lifeline and rolled into the boat.

"What's the matter?" Tapscott demanded, still clutching the side.

"I'm not going. I don't want to. Not now," Widdicombe said.

"Well, I'm not if you're not," Tapscott said, indignantly, and he, too, dragged himself back into the boat.

There seemed some hope of a breeze. They got up the sail. It hung empty at the mast. The boat washed lazily, this way and that, under the breathless, stifling sky. Low black clouds were massing on the horizon, but they did not care. The sun burned down and the sea sent back a cruel glitter into their unseeing eyes. They gulped painfully for breath, their sides heaving, their blackened tongues protruding from their swollen, discolored mouths.

Toward noon Widdicombe was seized with another violent cramp. He rolled and rocked in the bottom of the boat until the seizure passed. He lay exhausted for some minutes, then said to Tapscott: "Let's go."

"O.K.," said Tapscott from the port seat.

Widdicombe lowered himself over the side and clung to the lifeline. Tapscott rolled over. His body struck the water with a splash. He schooled himself to lie still. Automatically, he floated. The cool water seemed to be saturating him; the shock stung his deadened nerves into action. He looked up from the water, shaking the long hair out of his eyes. He was five or six feet behind the boat. Widdicombe was still clinging to the lifeline.

"Come on," Tapscott called.

Widdicombe gave no sign of hearing.

"Let go," Tapscott said.

Widdicombe did not move.

"Well, to hell with him," Tapscott said to himself, and went into a laborious crawl. He was surprised that he could swim so well. When he came alongside the boat again he said: "Why don't you let go?"

Widdicombe shook his head violently.

Tapscott felt a rush of rage. Widdicombe wasn't playing fair! Had he not looked up from the water when he did, a minute or two more, and it would have been too late. The hell with Widdicombe! He, too, took hold of the lifeline.

Hanging from the rope Tapscott and Widdicombe argued the matter. Having once made up his mind, Tapscott was determined to go. But he wasn't going without Widdicombe.

Widdicombe excused his failure to go through with the agreement on the ground that his pain had passed. Whether it was the effect of the water or a natural eventuality, he felt much better. Immersion was making Tapscott feel much better, too.

"If you're strong enough to swim that far," Widdicombe said, "you're strong enough to go on some more."

Tapscott reflected that this was true. By this time he was quite willing to be convinced. The very fact of swimming seemed to give him new confidence in his ability to carry on. He allowed himself to be persuaded without too much difficulty. Together, and with much effort, they got themselves back into the boat again.

Together they crawled back under the boat cover. They felt that they had been accorded a new lease on life. But as the sun drew overhead and the water dried on their bodies, leaving them rimy with salt, their suffering recommenced.

Tapscott, who thought that he must be suffocating, was taken with an idea. The only liquid in the boat was in the compass. It was not water, it was true, but it was not salty. Why not drink it? The idea had occurred to them before, but always they had put it resolutely from

Tapscott and Widdicombe, shaved, fed and dressed in new clothes, on arrival in Nassau. *Arthur K. Blood*

Widdicombe points to notches in gunwale of the jolly-boat. *Stanley Toogood*

them; on the compass depended their ability to reach land by the shortest possible route. But now all considerations, however weighty, were as nothing to that of relieving, if only for an instant, the raging torment of thirst.

They got out the compass and stared avidly at the clear, colorless liquid in which the card floated. Tapscott found the hole closed with a screw cap, by which it was filled. He unscrewed the cap and decanted the alcohol into two condensed-milk tins that served them for cups. He divided it exactly; they had about three-quarters of a water glass each. Tapscott refilled the compass with sea water. So far as he could see it operated successfully on that.

"Remember those old men and women under the canal bridge at home? They drink this stuff. I never thought I'd be doing it," Tapscott said.

As if standing each other a go in a Newport pub they sat opposite each other on the thwarts and drank the alcohol. It rasped their raw throats and burned their intestines. They did not care. It was liquid and at the very first drop their bodies responded with a start.

Several swallows, and they grinned at each other. Peril and pain were forgotten. A blissful oblivion was stealing through their veins.

They sat there drinking. They laughed and ragged each other in strange, throaty croaks, their misshapen mouths grinning like gargoyles. They recalled famous binges in foreign ports. Tapscott told of a Norwegian in Barcelona harbor who, while stone drunk, had dived off the bridge to win a bet of five bob with the Old Man. They said nothing of the *Anglo-Saxon*, nothing of their present situation.

When the alcohol was gone they rolled over and went to sleep. It was the first uninterrupted and completely relaxed sleep they had had since leaving their blazing ship.

Six hours or more later they woke up. It was night. There was no moon, no stars. The air was thick and hard to breathe. A pall of black cloud hung over them, near enough, it seemed, to touch. If they had been thirsty before, this must be the very apogee of thirst, thanks to the alcohol. Their heads throbbed and nausea racked them as the boat rose and fell.

They had no idea of their whereabouts, or even in what direction they were drifting. They had failed to put out the sea-anchor in their orgy of sleep; but, luckily, the sea was smooth and windless. They got the anchor over and stretched out on their seats.

Sometime toward morning, Tapscott, who had dozed off into a cat nap, was roused by a terrific peal of thunder. Lightening flashed on the horizon, throwing the clouds into livid relief. The surface of the sea showed a ghastly green for a moment; then all was dark again. The rumbling and muttering of thunder drew nearer. Balls of fire, a variety of lightning he had never seen before, flamed in the heavens. More clouds closed over them and a darkness so close it was impossible to see on the boat.

Tapscott peered uneasily ahead, wondering if squalls were bearing down on them. With a terrifying crash a tongue of lightning flickered down from the cloud mass and hissed into the sea. A moment later there was a splatter of drops on the boat cover.

They rolled themselves out from under the cover and stretched it across the thwarts. Rain! Now that it was here they disbelieved the fact of it; they had looked for it so long in vain. The drops became a shower and a puddle formed in the hollow of the canvas. They could not wait, but dipped their tins into it scraping the tin edges frantically into the grain of the canvas in their eagerness to drink. At the first swallow, they spat the water out. It was saltier than sea water. The boat cover was so impregnated with salt from the gallons of spray that had fallen on it the water was spoiled. Regretfully they drained the canvas over side and sat waiting for it to fill again.

They had collected a few mouthfuls when the shower ceased as suddenly as it had started. They threw themselves down in disgust, but did not despair. Surely there would be more rain. The very air smelt of it.

Toward dawn the rain came, a cloudburst of it. The skies opened and it sluiced down in steady, heavy sheets. It plastered their long hair to their skulls and their rags to their bodies, washing the salt out of them and filling the boat with almost fresh water.

With the cover spread again they soon had a good puddle in the middle of it. This time it was fresh. The first rain had washed the boat cover clean. They poured water down their throats by the canful, spilling it out of the corners of their mouths, down their chins and chests, with joyful, gluttonous, animal noises. Tapscott had drunk three canfuls when his stomach, constricted and unconditioned by the long drought, revolted and sent it all up again. After that he was cautious and took the water by sips. No man ever held an old wine in his mouth, savoring its bouquet as Tapscott did each mouthful of rainwater. He let it roll voluptuously round the root of his tongue, and, tilting back his head with infinite caution, let it trickle down his damaged throat. Never before had he known such pleasure in drink.

Widdicombe, who had not drunk as much as Tapscott at first, had no trouble keeping his water down.

Using the boat hook for a tool, Tapscott pried out the bow air-tight tank from its fastening. He cut a hole in the soft copper with the Mate's knife, making a bung in the top of it. They rigged a series of creases and run-offs and let the water drain off the canvas into the tank. Tapscott fashioned a plug for it from the loom of an oar. They caught about six gallons of water.

Their thirst quenched, Tapscott and Widdicombe were aware of hunger as a sensation apart from their general misery. It was the first recognizable hunger they had felt in days. They soaked sea biscuit in water and ate it.

By early afternoon the storm had passed and the rain ceased. A light breeze sprang up. Life flowed back into them. They were very weak, but the tide, definitely, had changed. Widdicombe was jubilant.

"I knew we'd make it," he declared. "I knew it the moment we got back into the boat. If we couldn't go then, it stands to reason that we're going to be O.K."

This was September 12th, their twenty-third day in the boat. Widdicombe got out the log. He had not touched it since Morgan went over the side. He wrote:

Sept. 12th. A cloudburst gave us water for six days.

II

WITH ALL the water they wanted going into their desiccated tissues, a quiet night behind them and the knowledge that there was more water in the tank, Tapscott and Widdicombe woke early the next morning and got under way.

A stiff breeze was blowing. The boat, as if answering to the general improvement in their situation, picked up speed.

"If this holds," Widdicombe said, "we'll make the Leeward Islands any day now."

They breakfasted on sea biscuit softened with water and felt surfeited on little of it.

Their skins, they noticed, had reacted curiously to the water; their bodies were covered with minute blisters, which broke when they passed their palms over them, covering them with sweat.

The sun was hotter now than it had been before and the character of the sea seemed to have changed. The water was bluer. Now and again they sighted clumps of floating seaweed. The sun was acutely uncomfortable outside the shelter, but they took their turns at the oar cheerfully enough. They had water at last and they were sure they would get more.

"I wish," Tapscott said, "we hadn't dumped the rest of that last tin of mutton overboard. If we'd put it in a wet cloth it might have kept."

"That's all right to say now, Widdicombe reminded him, "but you didn't want any of it then. You wouldn't touch it."

"That's not now," Tapscott said, ruefully.

"Never mind, Bobby," Widdicombe said. "We'll spend all of that pound note Sparks left us on dinner when we land."

Tapscott looked sourly at his boat mate. Of many things he disliked about Widdicombe his habit of calling him "Bobby," a name he detested, was one he resented most. And these swings up and down from windy optimism to darkest despair were contrary to his canon of conduct. It was all right in Latins and other foreigners, but no manner for a British sailor. But the thought of meat, fibrous, bulky, satisfying meat, was a pleasanter one and he clung to that. "Whatever he does or says," he told himself, "no matter how it gets on my nerves, I must put up with it until this show is over. We need each other to get through. It would be idiotic to fight. But . . ."

"The Mate figured we'd be in the steamer lanes a long time ago," Widdicombe said. "We'll probably be picked up before we make land."

"It's all one to me," Tapscott said, "as long as we eat."

The breeze held. The sun was the worst they had yet experienced. They bailed water over each other and shortened their tricks at the steering oar. The man in the sun stuck it as long as he could and then called for relief. He sheltered under the boat cover until the other man could stand it no longer. Thus they got through the day.

They lay to that night after having drunk all the water they wanted and having made a meal on softened sea biscuit. They knew they should ration the water, but their bodies had been so thoroughly dried out that they could not discipline themselves to deny them all they craved just yet. They were sure they would get more. And whether they did or not they could not do otherwise now. In the morning they noticed with surprise that their legs had swollen and that they were covered with a new crop of the tiny water blisters.

The next day was very like the day before, except that they talked a great deal more, mostly of food. They discussed it in all its forms and planned ideal meals. This only made them the more ravenous for meat, but they were so profoundly pleased to have cheated death from thirst they laughed at their hunger. They turned out Sparks' attaché case and scraped up the tobacco and lint in the bottom of it. They filled the pipe and managed a few whiffs each. It seemed indecently luxurious.

Nevertheless, when the sun went down that night they were greatly relieved. The quality of the heat seemed more punishing than that they had experienced farther east. The air was heavier, more humid. The direct rays of noon burned and stung like heated needles.

The breeze held all that day and the next. They drank all the water they craved.

"We're so near land now," Widdicombe said, "it doesn't make any difference."

But, on the morning of September 18th, they were becalmed. Worse, they had reached the bottom of the water tank again.

For two days they drifted this way. It did not seem so bad as before. They had learned a technique of suffering. They were unable to eat dry biscuit, and the horrible dryness was throttling them again. But they held on hopefully, confident that they would get rain.

It came early on the morning of the 20th. It was a good rain. They rigged the cover and run-offs. They drank copiously. Tapscott, having learned his lesson, took his water slowly. He had no trouble keeping it down.

While the tank was filling they soaked six biscuits each in rain water. When they were soft they ate them. Their supply was getting low, but they had been without food for two days. The rain did not last as long as they would have liked. Still, they had enough water for several days.

"By the time that's gone we'll have reached land," Widdicombe said confidently.

The biscuit tank was nearly empty now, so they decided to limit themselves to one biscuit a day. But they drank all the water they wanted.

Their stomachs swelled ludicrously with the food and water. They had sores on their hips from lying on the hard thwarts. In spite of life-belts as cushions these sores grew worse. They noted with some surprise that their bowels had started functioning again. They had a decent night's rest, which helped their morale enormously.

Widdicombe got out the log and wrote:

Sept. 20th. Rain again for four days. Getting very weak but trusting in God to pull us through.

W. R. Widdicombe
R. Tapscott.

They had no thought of sailing that night. If they were so near land, why hurry? They had no suspicion that miles and miles of Atlantic lay between them and the nearest land.

"Keep your eye peeled, Bobby," Widdicombe said. "We may see it any minute now."

Toward sunset on September 24th, they were sure that they had made landfall, a low, blue-black mass on the horizon. But as they drew nearer it shifted. Even then they were hopeful; a land mass gives the appearance of shifting sometimes with a boat's change of position. But when they had sailed a while longer they saw that it was cloud.

Several times they had arguments over this: a cloud mass that looked like land. It always revealed itself finally as mirage. They began to wonder what had gone wrong. They had held a course generally west. Even allowing for the aimless drifting they had done at times, wind and current could not have carried them anywhere but in the direction they wanted to go.

The next morning they up-ended the tank and dribbled the last of the water into their cans. They fumbled in the biscuit tank, but it yielded only broken bits and crumbs. They were without food and water.

Widdicombe fell into the deepest despondency. Fate had done him in the eye again! Water, he felt, they would get; but where would they get food?

No use giving up now, Tapscott said. They could take it. It couldn't go on this way much longer. He was hungry, it was true, very hungry, and both of them looked like scarecrows, but being without food was easy compared to being without water.

Widdicombe made a final entry in the log:

Sept. 24th. All water and biscuits gone. Still hoping to make land.

W. R. W.

Tapscott noticed that Sparks' razor kit contained a mirror. As they sailed and drifted, hungrily and thirstily the next day, he diverted himself by studying his face and features. He was shocked at first to see how his face had changed. His cheeks were flabby hollows and his cheek-bones knuckly protuberances. His nose, normally a substantial, fleshy organ, had shrunk to a bony ridge and two thin nostrils, changing his entire expression. He was amused at the way his beard grew, particularly the fringe on the lower surface of his chin and jaws. He decided that he looked like the stock fisherman in the *Punch* cartoons. He was concerned with the number of eruptions and blemishes that had come out on his face.

Tapscott was nineteen. At that age one's appearance is a matter of the greatest interest and importance. He spent many abstracted and interested periods with Sparks' mirror, then and during the long bad dream that followed. He was as grateful for it as a man on a desert island for one book.

During the muggy, stifling night the tension cracked and rain fell again. They had all they wanted to drink and collected a good tankful. The rain soaked them through and through, blanching and wrinkling their hands. It gathered in the boat and they were forced to bail.

When the sun rose, they stripped off their rags and put everything out to dry. The breeze lifted and they set sail. Had it not been for that gnawing vacuity in their middles they would have been gay.

Widdicombe was purposeful again.

"We'll have to sail nights," he said. "Something's wrong with our figuring. We should have made land by now."

They decided, too, that they had best ration the water. They agreed that three dipperfuls a day was about right.

They made good progress that day. When darkness came they did not lie to, but held their course. They took regular watches.

The boat sailed steadily in the starlit night, carrying them westward. As Tapscott sat in the stern sheets, holding the oar, giving an occasional glance at Arcturus or brilliant Jupiter and his satellite in their traverse of the sky, he thought of beef—thick, red, juicy, dripping slices of beef. He dozed off and then awoke with a guilty start. He must stay awake now. It helped to think of beef. What went best with it, a pint of bitter or a tankard of Irish ale?

12. THE LAST LAP

THE FIVE weeks that followed their reprieve from death—the last lap—were like a long, bad dream to Tapscott and Widdicombe. They remembered certain days, the one when a flying fish flew into the boat, for example, but there were stretches, when one day followed another in such an unvarying pattern of hunger, sun and sea, that they ran together, an indistinguishable blur in the continuity of their suffering.

There were periods of great clarity, under the stress of extreme danger, and long periods of stupor from heat and starvation. All of this time the rhythm of physical existence was slowing down. The subtle debility of slow starvation mounted in unmarked stages until it reached and sapped the very faculty of memory. Their last week in the boat was almost a blank to them.

The day and night following their decision to sail at night was distinguished by nothing but hunger. They were new to a total lack of food. The water they drank revealed as a special craving what had before been an indistinguishable element in their general sufferings.

They cast about the boat for something to eat, anything. There was nothing, nothing they could even think of chewing.

Tapscott had an idea.

"Why not seaweed?" he asked. They had passed clumps of it in considerable number and he remembered the succulent variety of it sold and eaten in Wales under the name of rock laver, which went very well, indeed, particularly when fried with the breakfast bacon.

They kept sharp watch for the next seaweed they should encounter. They were not long in finding it. But far from resembling the long, black, edible laver, which, soft as it is, had, at home, to be boiled in huge pots before being sold for further cooking, this sea weed was tough, rubbery and salty. It was covered with small, hard bulbs resembling berries. They snared a large bunch of it with the boat hook and stowed it in the bow-sheets. It gave them hours of chewing, but very little nourishment. It was impossible to reduce it to a pulp they could swallow without prolonged mastication. The salt in it, even when they had rinsed it in rain water, gave them intolerable thirst.

The seaweed was not very successful as food; but it was better than nothing.

The next night something happened that fixed the period indelibly in Tapscott's mind. It was morning, to be exact, for the stars he checked on had passed the celestial meridian and he was dozing in the stern sheets in the last half hour of his watch.

The boat grounded! At least, that was Tapscott's first thought when he was jarred out of his doze. The bow had encountered something solid. It had risen gently and had practically stopped. Second thought told him that it was impossible to ground in deep ocean. He considered what to do. Widdicombe was snoring under the boat cover. Tapscott decided to go forward and investigate.

A mighty stir under his feet and the boat, sliding backward at a sharp angle, settled all this. The water boiled and heaved; the boat dropped back into it, rocking violently. Twenty feet or so away a huge fluke broke water, threshed the sea with one mighty stroke, and disappeared. They had grounded on a whale!

Widdicombe, roused by the commotion, thought that Tapscott had lost his mind. Grounded on a whale, indeed! There were no whales in this part of the ocean. He studied his companion suspiciously and asked him how he felt.

"All right," said Tapscott sullenly. "I know a whale when I see one."

He crawled under the boat cover in a huff and Widdicombe took his place at the steering oar.

Tapscott could not sleep. Some time later he thought he heard a thud against the sail, another on the boat cover over him, and a desperate flapping in the boat. They had seen flying fish in schools but none had come very near them. He was sure, now, that one of them had barged into the sail and was somewhere in the boat. He fumbled for the Mate's torch, which still gave forth a sickly glow, and looked for his quarry. He could find no trace of it. He decided, regretfully, that it had flopped overboard. He went back under the boat cover to sleep.

The next morning, remembering the fish, Tapscott made a thorough search for it. To his incredulous joy he found it, wedged between two battens at the bottom of the boat. He got out Sparks' razor and cut it in two. He took the head half. Widdicombe had the other. They ate it all, every scrap, eyes, bones and fins.

What maddened them was that there were fish all about now. Small ones swam alongside them for hours. They saw dorsal fins. One large fish, which they were convinced was a shark, came up boldly alongside. Widdicombe thrust at it with an oar.

Widdicombe dabbled his fingers over side. The larger fish came to this dangerous bait. He stabbed at them with the Mate's knife. He spent fruitless hours at this and was never able to do more than

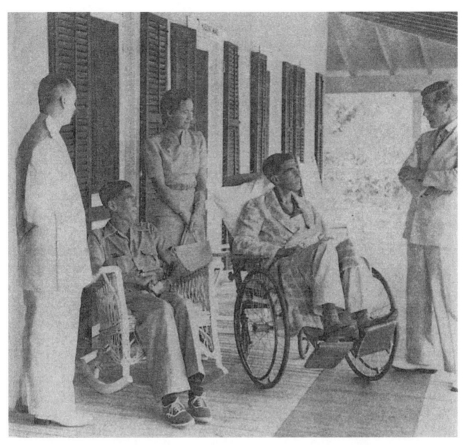

The Duke and Duchess of Windsor visit Tapscott and Widdicombe at Nassau Hospital.

Tapscott and Widdicombe sail the jolly-boat in Nassau Harbor. *Stanley Toogood*

wound one of them. They became an obsession with him. When they reappeared near the boat he cursed and swore at them, defying them to come within fair stroke of his knife.

The next morning they saw an impressive sight. A whole gam of whales appeared off to the starboard, ten or twelve of them. They cruised along serenely, apparently unaware of the boat, or, if aware of it, completely undisturbed. Tapscott and Widdicombe watched them with respect and apprehension. Suppose one of these huge creatures should take it into his head to charge them? They said nothing until the whole shoal had safely distanced the boat. Then Widdicombe apologized for having doubted Tapscott's story of the other night. He was overcome with belated awe that they had got off as easily as they had when they grounded on one.

Neither Tapscott nor Widdicombe knew enough about whales to identify the species. All that they could report was that they were long-headed, about twenty feet long over all, and that they did not spout.

The next day was without incident. Their initial supply of seaweed had dried out and they saw none that day. They chewed the hardened, leathery strings for hours; but, chew as they might, hunger was now an active torture.

"I wonder what became of that little fish," Tapscott said.

Several days before they grounded on the whale they had seen a small, pinkish object come over the gunwale in a sea.

"It must be somewhere about," Tapscott said, groping on his knees.

He searched the boat systematically, coiling rope, folding the boat cover, stacking the sodden life-belts, stowing the sea-anchor and generally tidying up. He bailed the boat laboriously, finally finding what he was looking for. The fish was small, soft and rotten; but they ate it, gladly.

"An odd taste it had," Tapscott said, "rather coppery."

After eating the spoiled fish they feared they had poisoned themselves. They waited for the symptoms to appear. Tapscott did feel some qualms in his stomach, but they passed. Widdicombe was unaffected.

Now they were encountering great patches of seaweed. They got a large supply of it aboard and were delighted to find a tiny variety of crab in its meshes. There were, also, some small shellfish, rather like the winkles they got at the seaside resorts at home, which one ate with the aid of a pin. They winnowed out a large number of these, but it took handfuls to make a decent mouthful.

In searching Sparks' attaché case for an implement with which to extract the meat from their shellfish, Tapscott found a safety pin, which gave him another idea. He bent it into a hook, fixed it to a length of spun yarn he found in the boat, sacrificed half a crab for bait, and put it over the side. One of the big fish struck it almost immediately. He jerked the line, hooked his fish, and let out a howl of joy.

"Play him!" Widdicombe yelled, wild with excitement at the prospect of a real meal. "Play him up to the boat and I'll get him with the knife!"

But the metal of the pin was too soft. The fish gave an outraged leap, plunged, and the hook straightened out, releasing him. Furious, they bent the pin back into shape and tried again. They had another strike. Again they lost the fish; this time he wriggled off the barbless point. They tried over and over. They had no trouble getting strikes. But, always, the hook was too soft and their fish got away. Disgusted, they gave it up in the end.

Seaweed was their sole source of food. The patches of it were growing larger in area daily. They scorned the small detached clumps now, waiting until they sighted a floating field of it. Sometimes there were leads through it, like open water in an ice floe. When they found one of these they steered the boat into it. Moving slowly, they picked crabs, winkles and anything that seemed edible out of it.

The seaweed patches they were now encountering contained a small shrimp as well as crabs and winkles. These were a most welcome addition to their diet—if such it could be called—but, like the crabs, were too small to supply much substance. Hours of work were required to furnish a meal. Unsatisfied after such labor, and after dark, they picked over their supply of seaweed in the boat for the most tender morsels and chewed on that.

The weather held generally fair until October 8th. Except for their side excursions into kelp fields and the extra mileage on tacks they made good progress westward. Late that day, however, squalls blew up, and rain. They lay to, spreading the boat cover and the sail over them in an attempt to keep dry. They passed a damp but, by comparison with some others during the trip, comfortable night.

Day broke overcast and drizzling. They decided to stay as they were until the weather lifted. They had already collected all the water they needed. There was nothing to do but sleep. Widdicombe was still snoring when Tapscott wakened. Rain was drumming on the canvas over them. Tapscott lifted the canvas, sat up, and looked about. The sky was leaden and the visibility poor. There was some swell on the sea. He checked the sea-anchor and found it in order. He was about to pull the canvas over him again when his glance, roving aft, fixed on a sight that riveted his eyes. Not more than a half mile away, off the port bow, bearing southerly, was a large steamer.

"Roy! Roy!" he yelled, shaking Widdicombe savagely. "A ship!"

Widdicombe sat up sleepily. He did not take it in for a minute. Tapscott was already heaving in the sea-anchor. Together they got it in, grabbed oars and rowed frantically toward her.

Pulling as hard as they could, the steamer was distancing them. They rowed until they could go on no longer. They stood up in the boat, waving their arms and shouting. The steamer showed no signs of seeing them. They swung their oars, semaphore fashion, and Tapscott, finding the Mate's whistle, stood up in the bow and blew it until he was breathless. The liner steamed steadily ahead.

They picked up their oars again and tried to row to it. They were so weak and winded they achieved only a few strokes. Tapscott seized the whistle and blew it as hard and as long as he could. The liner kept her course. Then, turning sharply, she went off east.

Tapscott and Widdicombe collapsed on their oars, completely spent. Their hearts were beating as if to burst; their lungs heaved and they gulped down air in sobbing spasms. When they had recovered enough to handle the boat, they put it about and hoisted sail. Sick with disappointment and fatigue, they resumed their course west.

13. HURRICANE ZONE

FOR FOUR days after losing the passenger liner the weather was unsettled. The wind shifted about the compass uneasily. Rain squalls struck Tapscott and Widdicombe from unexpected quarters and the sea lost its reliable northeasterly swell. Confused winds and choppy cross waves buffeted them about, making steering difficult and exhausting. They shipped a great deal of water and had to bail at all hours. They noticed when bailing how much weaker they had become. They tired quickly and had to take more frequent rests.

Toward sunset of the fourth day the wind fell away and the sun appeared for a few minutes. It shone wanly through a brownish haze, which turned a sickly yellow as the sun sank lower. The sunset sky was lighted with a disturbing greenish glare. The air lay heavy and the sea ran in long sullen swells under lowering and massy clouds.

With darkness came a cold drizzle. They decided to lie to for the night. Wrestling with the steering oar had worn them out. They put out the sea-anchor, lashing together their spare oars and adding them to it as an extra precaution against the uncertainty of the weather. They fastened down the boat cover as best they could and spread the sail over that. Rain flurries blew down on them in fitful gusts, but they remained fairly dry.

Some time after midnight, Tapscott judged, he was awakened by the howl of wind and the violent tossing and pitching of the boat. The sea had risen and was running in high dangerous waves. The oars and sea-anchor were holding them into it but there was something in the changed motion of the boat that filled him with apprehension. It seemed to be lower in the water and to have lost buoyancy.

"Roy," Tapscott said, groping across the boat toward Widdicombe, "wake up!"

"What?" Widdicombe asked, drowsily.

"Show the light," Tapscott said.

"What?" Widdicombe repeated.

Tapscott dropped his hand down into the boat. It touched water almost instantly.

"We're filling!" he said.

Widdicombe got the torch and clicked it on. In the faint light they saw water within a few inches of the thwarts. At that moment the crest of one of the large waves caught them flush on the bow and the sea poured in over the gunwales. Tapscott seized the bucket and Widdicombe a can, and they started bailing. Another sea like that, and they would have been swamped. They worked quietly and desperately, thanking God for the two remaining air-tight tanks. They did not seem to be making an impression on the water in the boat. Another ten minutes of bailing as fast as they could move, and they saw the level drop. Their hearts were thumping alarmingly and they gasped for breath.

A blast of wind, fiercer than anything they had yet experienced, struck them astern, driving the boat ahead of it. High waves followed in rapid succession as if intent upon burying them under tons of water.

"We'll have to run for it," Widdicombe said.

The reefed the sail, got everything in readiness and waited for a favorable chance to hoist and run. Timing their effort to the rhythm of the waves they eased in the sea-anchor, got the boat about and hauled sail part way up the mast. The howling gale caught the reefed lug. The boat careened crazily and drove forward. They thanked God for the rolling chocks on the clinkered bottom and the life-boat lines of their boat. Even under their scrap of sail they were heeled over dangerously, tearing through broken seas and flying foam.

Dawn came as a lightening in a leaden sky. Ragged bits of cloud flew before the northeast gale. Screeching blasts whooped down on them, blowing off the tops of the towering waves and blasting them with spindrift that stung like shot. The boat raced ahead of it, and, luckily, ahead of the following sea.

"My God!" Tapscott exclaimed as he looked back. A wave, twenty feet high, was speeding down on them, its crest curling over. It broke, right over them it seemed. Tons of water crashed just behind them and the boat shot forward, staggering as if run into by a speeding train.

It took both of them to manage the steering oar. Ahead was a howling, tumbling chaos of wind and water; behind, huge racing waves. They dared not look back. It was too terrifying. They needed all their heart and courage for this.

When the boat started to lift they knew that a wave had caught up with them. They prayed for inertia enough to permit it to pass and not tumble them end over end or broached to under it. Once sideways to one of these seas, they would be finished, rolled over and over like a toy in the surging power of the breaking crest.

Up, up, up they went, the sea falling away before them until they hung over a sickening depth. A horrible moment of waiting and they were racing down the watery steep like a toboggan, certain to plunge under the water or be buried by the breaking monster behind. But once in the rough they leveled off, held for a moment, and started to rise again.

At other times a side blast struck them like the concussion of an exploding bomb, hurling them sideways. They held on grimly, blinded, gagged and drenched by the flying spray and rain; their mouths filled with water, sometimes salt, sometimes fresh.

All day they fought the storm, too occupied to think of anything but the peril of the moment, holding the bucking and leaping boat to its course. At nightfall the wind eased a bit and they felt better for not being able to see the waves. They could judge events only by the lift and fall of the boat, or when some charging monster broke near them, flooding the sea with phosphorescent foam.

There was no question of sleep. They did not dare lie to, and it took both of them to manage the oar. Drenched, cold and dog-tired they huddled in the stern-sheets. Every little while one of them had to bail.

The second day of the storm dawned a dirty gray with the wind howling demoniacally, but blowing more steadily. The sea was higher and less confused. Waves thirty and forty feet high raced behind them but with some order in their periods. The boat raced with them, driven at express speed.

"At any rate," Widdicombe said grimly, "we're making time." His face was livid and his eyes rolled wildly showing the whites as they did in moments of excitement.

Tapscott was so exhausted he fell asleep for minutes, sitting bolt upright at the oar. He did not sleep long; stinging douches of flying salt water and gusts of rain shocked him into consciousness.

They noted with relief as the day wore on that the wind was dropping. The rain ceased, and late that afternoon the sun appeared for a few minutes through the torn vault of massy black cloud. They had no sense of hunger; they were too frightened for that. But asked later if this was the time of his greatest fear during the trip, Tapscott said, no; he was frightened every minute of it.

Water, however, they could not do without. When they drank some from the tank, they discovered that it was slightly salt. Some of the gallons of falling spray had driven in around the ill-fitted bung. But it was not too tainted to drink.

They spent another night of riding tremendous waves and steady bailing. But the wind was abating. They hoped desperately for a better morrow. They were about at the end of their strength.

The rising sun revealed a turbulent sea, but one they could safely lie to in. They got over the sea-anchor and lashed oars and fell exhausted upon the side seats. They slept this way until noon, when the heat of the sun awakened them again.

The wind was fresh but steady now. They stripped off their scanty clothes and spread them to dry. Naked, they got under way again. The sun was frequently obscured by the breaking clouds, but they were warm and refreshed. They chewed on the seaweed and drank their ration of slightly salty water. They looked at each other and grinned; another great danger successfully passed.

That night they went back to their system of watches and both of them got some sleep.

14. NIGHTMARE

FOOD WAS Tapscott's and Widdicombe's first thought on awakening to the new day. The sun was warm, the breeze fair and the sea placid. Their bodies cried for sustenance, substance to digest.

They scanned the sea for something to eat—anything. They sailed until they sighted a patch of seaweed and made for it. They snatched at the bunches and trailers, fingering it avidly, hunting for something edible. They found some small crabs.

Tapscott restrained himself until he had three crabs clutched in his fist, then crammed them into his mouth. One of them escaped the first crunch of his teeth. Wriggling frantically, it nearly forced its way out of his mouth. One of its legs stuck out from between his lips. He forced it back with his hand and chewed savagely. The wriggling in his mouth stopped.

But this seaweed contained few crabs and winkles. They became frantic. They stripped the peeling skin from their bodies and ate that.

They chewed the toughest seaweed. They tore the latex lining from Sparks' tobacco pouch and chewed on that. It gave them nothing in the way of nourishment, but they had the illusion of eating and it kept their mouths moist.

They were very light-headed now. The lag between thought and the execution of the simplest movement was longer than it had been at the time when they were near death from thirst earlier in the trip. They sat for hours saying nothing, thinking of nothing but things they could chew or swallow.

For seven days they went on in this manner.

The weather had changed. The winds were lighter, the sea calmer and the sun hotter. The water was clearer and bluer. Great cloud banks piled up on the horizon as tangible as white marble, and fleets of cloud ships cruised majestically across the sky.

Several times they thought they saw land. Toward sunset or early in the morning a low-lying cloud bank seemed as solid and immobile as an island. In their trance-like condition, however, neither of them mentioned it when they thought they saw land. They waited until the breeze had dispersed it or their own eyes proved it to be a mirage.

They could no longer stand on their feet. They pulled themselves about the boat with their hands or crawled on all fours. They gave up trying to keep watches and sail nights. They adjusted their sleep to the breeze. If it held into the night they sailed with it. If it dropped, they slept. It was gentle enough now to drift for hours before it without troubling to steer.

Widdicombe suffered more and more from the sun. His spells of hysteria were more frequent. He sat for hours apparently neither hearing nor seeing. Tapscott himself was often giddy and caught himself babbling incoherent and unintentional things.

As their suffering increased each man withdrew deeper into his individuality. At times Tapscott found Widdicombe glowering at him with unveiled hostility. He, in turn, found himself speculating with pleasure on the thought of giving Widdicombe a first-class beating.

It was plain to both of them that they could not go on much longer. They were skin and bone, having lost from seventy-five to eighty pounds each. The eruptions on their bodies had spread. They felt as if their entrails were shrinking away.

Between long periods of dazed torpor they had moments of great clarity. It seemed to Tapscott that, if anything, his mind was clearer then than it had ever been. Listening to Widdicombe inveighing against fate or regarding with distaste his trick of twisting his lips and jerking his head—tricks of manner he had disliked from the moment he met Widdicombe—he told himself he must forget it. On Widdicombe depended his life and on him Widdicombe's life depended. They must see this thing through together. He could carry on, he was sure; but how much longer could his body sustain the effort?

Widdicombe was visibly failing. He could not face the sun for any length of time. More and more he called on Tapscott to relieve him of the steering oar, often five or ten minutes after having taken over. Tapscott brooded on this. Maybe Widdicombe was ill; but he was weak, too. *He* did not call for relief directly he had taken over. The old suspicion that Widdicombe was evading work at his expense rankled in his tortured brain.

On the morning of October 27th, just after having started for the day, Widdicombe, whose turn it was, complained of dizziness and called to Tapscott to relieve him. Tapscott studied Widdicombe intently and decided he was speaking the truth. He took the oar and Widdicombe stretched himself out on one of the side seats. In a few minutes he was snoring.

After three hours at the helm, or thereabouts, as near as he could judge it, Tapscott called for relief. Widdicombe stirred, opened his eyes and heard Tapscott repeat his request. He rolled over again and paid no attention to it.

"All right, then," Tapscott said, shipping the oar. "Let the bloody boat sail itself. I'm through."

He left the stern sheets and made his way to the middle of the boat, where he sat down, braced against a thwart. Widdicombe, alongside him, watched him with narrowed eyes. He sat up slowly, his jaw jutted out. Tapscott had seen that expression before—the night Widdicombe had slugged Elliott. He was certain Widdicombe was about to hit. Before he could, Tapscott, gathering up all his remaining strength, punched Widdicombe flush on the jaw. Widdicombe went down on the seat, but was up a moment later flinging himself upon Tapscott. They rolled about in the bottom of the boat weakly pummeling each other. Suddenly, Widdicombe quit.

"I'm too weak," he said.

Tapscott pulled himself up on a thwart and waited. He did not relax his guard until Widdicombe had crawled aft and manned the steering oar.

They sailed and drifted for a long time without moving or speaking. Tapscott was feeling sorry now. He had not wanted to hit Widdicombe, but he was certain that it had been self-defense. Still, they were absolutely dependent upon each other. And when Tapscott thought of what they had been through and of the chaps who were gone, he was sorrier still.

"I'm sorry, Roy," he said, finally. "I'm sorry I hit you. It's crazy for us to fight."

Widdicombe grunted but said nothing. His lips were puffed and discolored from Tapscott's blow.

All that day, part of the night and until midnight the next day, they made fair progress. They said little or nothing, communicating when necessary by signs and grunts. It was an effort to talk and in spite of Tapscott's apology, feeling between them was strained.

To Tapscott it seemed as if they were moving in a child's dream of impotence, when he wants desperately to run, jump, hit or cry out and his body refuses to obey the command of his brain.

At midnight the wind fell away completely. They let the boat drift with the current and slept, not troubling even to lower the sail. Some time between then and dawn Tapscott thought he heard a fish flapping in the boat. The night was dark, the Mate's torch had gone dead and he was too weak to look for it. He decided to wait until daylight.

With the first light of dawn Tapscott was in the bottom of the boat, looking for the fish. He found it; what he called a gar. Actually it was a Bahamian hound fish, a long needlelike creature, almost transparent, which is considered inedible by the natives. Hound fish lie near the surface of the sea and when frightened leap clear out of it. An enemy had chased it into the boat.

"I've found it," Tapscott said.

Widdicombe said nothing.

"I've found the fish," Tapscott repeated, looking up to see why Widdicombe received this important news so apathetically. Widdicombe was staring straight ahead, his eyes straining from the sockets. "Look," he said, pointing.

Tapscott, holding the fish firmly, raised himself on a thwart to see. Dead ahead lay a long line of lowland and beach, stretching north and south, apparently, as far as they could see.

They had been deceived so many times before, they did not dare to believe it.

"Land?" said Tapscott.

Widdicombe nodded.

"You're sure we're not seeing things?"

Widdicombe shook his head. The breeze was rising and the boat picked up way. As they drew nearer, they could see a line of reef with the sea breaking over it. Those rocks and the spray they threw up were no mirage.

"It *is* land, Bobby," Widdicombe said, sounding as if he were about to cry. "It must be the Leeward Islands."

Tapscott stared and stared at the reef and the beach beyond. There was no doubt in his mind now. Had the night lasted longer or the wind held the night through, they would have sailed right into it. Suddenly a wrenching pain racked his bowels. Still staring at the land, he grabbed for the bucket that served them as latrine.

15. RESCUE

A LINE of reef and broken water separated them from the land. They could see bush in back of the beach, and, in places, clumps of higher bush or trees, but no sign of human habitation.

"Land or no land," Tapscott said, "I'm going to eat this fish."

He cut it in half with Sparks' razor and together they ate it, staring at the land.

When they had finished the fish, they stood up unsteadily and studied the water ahead.

"I think I see a place to get through," Tapscott said, indicating a patch of smooth water. They got in the sea-anchor, set sail and steered for it. It was a channel right enough, but extremely narrow. Tapscott lay in the bow and directed their course.

They threaded their way through patches of shoal and sharp rocky heads. It was easy to see them; the water was the clearest Tapscott had ever seen. It was the most brilliantly colored he had ever seen, too, ranging from ultramarine in the depths to aquamarine in the shallows. Below him, around rocky drops and coral-encrusted banks, brilliantly colored fish swam and long, purple sea-fans waved with the movement of the water. Here and there were patches of grass, and white sand between the rocks. He saw reticulated coral mounds like gargantuan brains. White trees of the same substance grew in this sea-garden.

Twenty minutes later the bow of their boat grounded on the beach. Tapscott clambered over the bow, surprised at his strength. Widdicombe followed with the boat hook. He had some idea of mooring the boat to it, driven in the beach. The tide was ebbing, but they did not know it at the time. They were on land!

The sun beat down on the white sand. In the lee of the bush there was shade. Like drunken men they staggered up the beach to it and collapsed. The effort of walking was too much for them.

They lay in the shade until Widdicombe was feeling better. He proposed that they start northward up the beach. He felt that they might find human beings there. Tapscott got to his feet with infinite effort. Now that they were actually on land, all his remaining strength seemed to have gone from him. Laboriously they started up the beach. Thirty or forty feet of walking and Tapscott collapsed. The job he had been carrying on by sheer will power and momentum was through.

How long Tapscott and Widdicombe lay on the edge of the bush they could not say. They were roused by the sound of blows somewhere in the bush in back of them. Someone was cutting a way through. Then they heard voices. They saw no one, but they knew someone was here, someone who retreated precipitously.

"They speak English whoever they are," Widdicombe said. "I heard them say 'fetch.'"

Tapscott was beyond answering.

"We'd better get back to the boat. They'll be coming back and might miss us," Widdicombe said. "Can you make it?"

Tapscott indicated that he would try.

They staggered and crawled back to a point on the edge of the bush opposite the boat. The tide had left it stranded. They lay there for a long time; then they heard voices again. The voices spoke English, an English such as they had never heard before, but, indubitably, English. A moment later, a colored man, a woman and several more colored men emerged from the bush and stood over them.

"Who you are?" one of them asked.

"English," Widdicombe said. "Off the *Anglo-Saxon.* Our ship was sunk by a German raider. We got away in the boat."

"When dat?" the man asked, dubiously.

"August 21st," Widdicombe said. "We were 65 days in the boat. We're starving."

A chorus of exclamations went up.

"Save me, Lawd!"

"Hey, man?"

"Today's the 25th, isn't it?" Widdicombe said.

"Today's the 30th," one of the men said.

"Then it's seventy days."

The group seemed suspicious. Nobody stirred.

"Look," said Widdicombe, taking Sparks' wallet from his pocket and handing it to the nearest man. "Papers."

The man took the wallet and extracted the log sheets and other papers from it. He studied them a long time and handed them to the others to look at.

Tapscott only half heard all this. He lay with closed eyes.

The spokesman was satisfied with what he read. He said something to the others. Neither Tapscott nor Widdicombe understood. The group broke into fresh exclamations of wonder and commiseration. The seamen knew they were safe.

"You can walk?" the spokesman said to Widdicombe.

Widdicombe tottered to his feet, but Tapscott could not rise. Two men lifted him by the arms. Supporting him on either side, with two men doing the same for Widdicombe, they started back through the bush. Tapscott managed a few steps, then crumpled up. Widdicombe gave it up, too.

The rescuing party held a consultation. Some of them went ahead; two picked up Tapscott and Widdicombe, pick-a-back, and followed. When they had gone ahead some distance in this fashion, one of the men who had gone ahead returned carrying a string of coconuts. He lopped off the ends of two with his machete and offered them to the rescued men. They both took long draughts of the milk and felt greatly refreshed. Tapscott dug at the meat of his with his nails and ate it.

More men came with supplies. One had a bottle of whiskey. He gave Tapscott a drink, but the smell of the liquor sickened him and he could not take it. He was then offered a bottle of beer, which he drank gratefully. Never had beer, his favorite drink, tasted better. It was as if the quintessence of all the beer he had ever drunk was distilled into that one glass. They gave him a bottle of sweet soda and he drank that.

When they had drunk they were given bully beef and sweet biscuits. Tapscott tore at his voraciously, but Widdicombe ate but little. Tapscott would have eaten more had they not stopped him. As it was, he consumed most of a tin of bully beef and a great many sweet biscuits. They were afraid he would make himself ill. He *was* feeling ill from the food, but he did not care.

After they had eaten, they lay back and rested, their eyes closed. Their rescuers made plans for their transportation. They understood that a truck lay somewhere ahead; that they were to be carried to it through the bush. Tapscott heard very little of this; he was faint and dizzy. Widdicombe, however, put them unreservedly in their rescuers' hands.

As Tapscott lay there, he was aware of someone's glance. He opened his eyes to see the woman they had first seen on the beach looking down at him with compassion and great concern. During the last days of the trip he had removed his khaki shorts and given them to Widdicombe, whose trousers were completely gone. Tapscott had underwear shorts and had finished the trip in them. They were now ripped and worn to a point where they defeated modesty. The woman had safety pins in her hand. With a quick movement and deft fingers she repaired the damage.

When they had rested adequately, their rescuers took Tapscott and Widdicombe on their backs again and carried them through the bush to a white road in which stood a truck. They lay prone in the body of the truck while it rattled and banged northward over a rudimentary road. They were given more beer and soda to drink.

The truck reached Governor's Harbor, the capital of Eleuthera, at two o'clock in the afternoon. They saw a small island connected to the mainland by a causeway on which were white houses, palm trees and casuarinas. There was a snug harbor, between the smaller island and the land, in which fishing boats rode quietly at anchor. As they rumbled down the causeway to the small cay, upon which was the older part of the settlement, including the administration buildings and most of the business houses, a crowd streamed out to meet them.

Surrounded by the crowd, they were taken to the house of Michael Gerassimos, the Commissioner. The Commissioner, who had already been informed of their landing, shook hands with them and congratulated them upon their exploit. He directed that they be taken to the Ross home, where they were put to bed.

In the large, old-fashioned double bed Tapscott lay back immobile. He could not sleep, however. A feeling of tense incredulity kept his nerves taut. At moments he wondered whether it were not all hallucination. The boat, the sun, hunger, thirst and the sea were the sole realities. He was so tired, though, he was satisfied to lie back with his eyes closed, moving only to take the tomato juice, water and other liquids they were given.

Widdicombe, however, could not lie still. He sat up talked, gesticulated and shifted restlessly. He wanted to see people.

Outside the old house a crowd of islanders, winter visitors and people from the boats milled about, hoping for a glimpse of the men who had escaped the German raider and crossed the larger part of the Atlantic Ocean in an open boat.

That evening Tapscott and Widdicombe had a light supper of cocoa, bread and butter. Tapscott had thought often of cocoa during the days of their worst hunger. He took it with delight and was surprised to find that the essential flavor of cocoa was so much stronger than he remembered. This seemed overpowering in its "cocoa-ness," even after he had poured sugar into his cup until the drink was a syrup. Neither of them could get enough sugar. They asked for and were given hard candy, which they sucked steadily.

At ten o'clock the Commissioner came and took their statement. He told them that H.R.H., the Duke of Windsor, the new Governor of the Bahamas, had been notified of their arrival. The Duke had given special instructions for their care and the conservation of the boat. They were to be removed to the Bahamas General Hospital the next day by plane. The Commissioner assured them, too, that radio messages had already been dispatched to England to notify their families of their miraculous escape. A crew of men had been sent to Alabaster Bay where they had landed, to bring in the boat.

When the commissioner had gone they tried to compose themselves for sleep. The house was quiet, the bed soft and they were exhausted. But the tension of mind, so at variance with the exhaustion of body, would not permit it. They smoked a good deal and listened to the buzzing of the mosquitoes.

At midnight, Dr. Francis Klein, Medical Officer at Eleuthera, himself a refugee from Hitler, came to give them a hasty examination. He had been in another part of the Island and had just returned. He found them suffering from pellagra. Their blood pressures were very low.

When the doctor had gone they again tried to sleep, with no better results than before. Tapscott lay still, his mind racing. Widdicombe threshed about in the bed. At intervals they smoked. Thus the night passed.

In the morning they had a breakfast of corn flakes, cocoa, bread and butter. Tapscott emptied the sugar bowl over his corn flakes. They did not seem too sweet. This surprised him, for, normally, he cared little for sweets.

After breakfast the Reverend William Hyslop, Methodist Missioner, came to cut their long hair and remove their fantastic beards. They were outfitted with underwear, white drill trousers, sports shirts and tennis shoes, all new.

All morning people came and went, local residents, American winter visitors and people from the other settlements who flocked in to see what the sea had cast up.

At noon a smart plane appeared over the harbor, circled and landed. A boat was sculled out to it and brought off Dr. J. M. Cruikshank, Chief Medical Officer, hatless and in white surgeon's coat, as if he had just stepped out of the hospital.

Tapscott and Widdicombe, washed, shaved, trimmed and clad in their new clothes were carried to a boat, sculled to the plane and put aboard. Several minutes later it took off.

Weak as they were, both Tapscott and Widdicombe were thrilled. It was their first trip in a plane. They saw beneath them opalescent waters, green cays, white shoals and blue deeps. This, indeed, Tapscott thought, was victory over the sea.

In what seemed a few minutes the hills, forts, towers, resort hotels, Government buildings and clustered pink and white houses of Nassau in their walled green gardens appeared below them. The plane circled and landed in the smooth water of the Pan-American Airport. A boat put out to them. They were lifted into it by huge colored men who handled them as easily as though they were children. The boat was sculled the few feet to the quay, where they were carried through a crowd of officials, newspapermen and townsfolk to a waiting ambulance. Ten minutes later they were in cool, crisp beds in the Bahamas General Hospital with white-coifed English nursing sisters and smart colored nurses giving them every attention known to their comforting craft.

Propped up in his bed alongside Widdicombe's, helpless as a baby, bloated and suffering internally from the food he had taken, Tapscott looked at Widdicombe from deep-sunken eyes. With lips that were like strips of discolored parchment, dried on the jaws of a skull, he smiled.

EPILOGUE

FOR EIGHT days Tapscott and Widdicombe were confined to their hospital room and not allowed to see anyone but doctors and nurses. Tapscott was in the worse condition. There was grave question, the first two days, whether he would be able to survive.

In addition to the effects of exposure, starvation and prolonged thirst, both suffered from pellagra. Their mental and nervous systems were badly deranged. They suffered from insomnia. Both were frequently hysterical or sunk in despondent apathy. Tapscott, who had held up so well in the boat, now had long spells of melancholia during which he wanted to die. Widdicombe seemed to recover his mental balance more rapidly than his stolid companion.

However, under the skillful treatment of Dr. J. M. Cruikshank, Chief Medical Officer, and his staff, the two young men improved, and on the eighth day their first visitors were H. R. H., the Duke of Windsor and the Duchess. From that time on, their recovery was rapid. Benefits were held for them and they enjoyed their hour of fame.

In February, Widdicombe was able to go home and went to New York to join a ship, the Furness-Prince liner, *Siamese Prince*. Although improving, Tapscott was not yet in shape to return to work. At the time this book goes to press, he is still in Nassau, the guest of the Governor.

The final irony of the epic fight for life, however, was reserved for Widdicombe. His fate is told in the following excerpt from a newspaper account appearing in the New York *Herald Tribune* of Thursday, February 27, 1941.

APPENDIX

Crew Aboard the SS *Anglo-Saxon*

Allnatt, Walter Robert Thomas Louis (Able Seaman). Merchant Navy. Age 28.

Bedford, George (Cook). Merchant Navy. Age 21.

Bresler, Adolphus (Able Seaman). Merchant Navy. Age 45.

Denny, Barry Collingwood (Chief Officer). Merchant Navy. Age 31. Son of C. Collingwood Denny and Alice Violet Denney.

Duncan, Alistair St. Clair (Second Officer). Merchant Navy. Age 28. Son of Johan S. Duncan of Burray, Orkney.

Eley, Albert (Fireman and Trimmer). Merchant Navy. Age 26. Son of Charles Eley and Amy Eley of Newport, Monmouthshire.

Elliott, Stanley George (Able Seaman). Merchant Navy. Age 22. Son of Mrs. A. Elliott of Blaina, Monmouthshire.

Flynn, Philip Robert Limpenny (Master). Merchant Navy. Age 53.

Son of Philip and Mary Flynn; husband of Monica Mary Flynn of Hove, Sussex.

Fowler, James (Greaser). Merchant Navy. Age 37. Son of Stephen Townsend Fowler and Elizabeth Fowler.

Gormley, James Joseph (Sailor). Merchant Navy. Age 24.

Green, Verdun Charles (Fireman and Trimmer). Merchant Navy. Age 24. Son of Albert and Rose Green; husband of Linda A. Green of Barry Dock, Glamorgan.

Hansen, Oscar Waldemar (Carpenter). Merchant Navy. Age 47. Son of Soren Peter and Mette Thomine Hansen of Newport, Monmouthshire.

Hawks, Lionel Henry (Third Engineer Officer). Merchant Navy. Age 23.

Houston, John Innes (Second Engineer Officer). Merchant Navy. Age 55. Son of Innes and Agnes Houston of Lisburn, Co. Antrim, Northern Ireland; husband of Mabel Ellen Houston of Romford, Essex.

Keyse, Trevor (Steward). Merchant Navy. Age 19. Son of James Robert and Margaret Keyse of Newport, Monmouthshire.

Maher, Thomas Francis (Boatswain). Merchant Navy. Age 34. Husband of Mary Ellen Maher of Cathays, Cardiff.

Milburn, Edward Ernest (Chief Engineer Officer). Merchant Navy. Age 39. Son of Edward Ernest and A. Milburn; husband of Ethel May Milburn of North Shields, Northumberland.

Morgan, Leslie Joseph (Assistant Cook). Merchant Navy. Age 20. Son of Charles and Gertrude Morgan of Newport, Monmouthshire.

Nicholas, Alfred John (Donkeyman). Merchant Navy. Age 37.

O'leary, Michael (First Radio Officer). Merchant Navy. Age 48. Husband of C. O'leary of Cleethorpes, Lincolnshire.

Oliver, Andres (Fireman and Trimmer). Merchant Navy. Age 26.

Peaston, John Daniel (Fireman and Trimmer). Merchant Navy. Age 29. Son of Mr. and Mrs. Edwin Henry Peaston.

Penny, Francis Graham (Marine). Age 44. Husband of Edith Elizabeth Penny of Eastney, Hampshire.

Pickford, Walter Murray (Third Officer). Merchant Navy. Age 30. Son of Comdr. G. T. Pickford, R.D., R.N.R., and D. I. M. Pickford.

Pilcher, Roy Hamilton (Second Radio Officer). Merchant Navy. Age 21. Son of Bernard A. and Beatrice H. Pilcher of Godalming, Surrey.

Prowse, William Frederick (Ordinary Seaman). Merchant Navy. Age 18. Son of Frederick W. and A. D. Prowse of Newport, Monmouthshire. His brother Ivor James also fell.

Rasmussen, (Fireman and Trimmer) Lars Christian. Merchant Navy. Age 53.

Rice, Thomas Albert (Fourth Engineer Officer). Merchant Navy. Age 20. Son of Thomas and Margaret Rice of Marsden, Co. Durham.

Savory, Robert (Sailor). Merchant Navy. Age 33. Son of William Lloyd Savory and of Mary Ellen Savory of Grimsby, Lincolnshire.

Smith, Alfred Ernest (Sailor). Merchant Navy. Age 41.

Stuart, Charles (Fireman and Trimmer) . Merchant Navy. Age 44. Son of John and Elizabeth Stuart.

Takle, Philip James (Ordinary Seaman). Merchant Navy. Age 16.

Tapscott, Robert (Sailor). Merchant Navy. Age 19.

Tenow, Frederick (Fireman and Trimmer). Merchant Navy. Age 58. Husband of Mary B. Tenow of Newport, Monmouthshire.

Tobin, M. (Fireman and Trimmer). Merchant Navy. Age 35.

Wallace, Charles John (Fireman and Trimmer). Merchant Navy. Age 21. Son of Charles and Catherine Wallace of Newport, Monmouthshire.

Ward, George William (Assistant Steward). Merchant Navy. Age 20. Son of Samuel and Ann Mercy Ward of South Shields, Co. Durham.

Widdicombe, Wilbert (Sailor). Merchant Navy. Age 21.

Williams, David (Fireman). Merchant Navy. Age 43.

Williams, David John (Fireman and Trimmer). Merchant Navy. Age 20. Son of Frederick and Margaret Williams of Barry Dock, Glamorgan.

Willis, Harry Alfred (Chief Steward). Merchant Navy. Age 40. Husband of A. M. Willis of Newport, Monmouthshire.

Seven Initial Survivors of the Attack on the SS Anglo-Saxon

Denny, Barry, C.

Hawks, Lionel H.

Morgan, Leslie J.

Penny, Francis G.

Pilcher, Roy H.

Tapscott, Robert G.

Widdicombe, Roy W. C.

Last Survivors

Tapscott, Robert G.

Widdicombe, Roy W. C.

INDEX

Italicized page numbers indicate
   illustrations.

Adventurers, 5
amputations, 68–69
Anglo-Saxon (freighter)
   crew of, 27–29, 30–31, 31–32, 136–39
   description, 27–28
   destination, 32
   night of attack, 34–42
   Tapscott's foreboding about, 25
   wartime conditions and shipping
      precautions, 31–32
Atlantic Ocean, map of route, *xi*

Bahama Islands. *See also* Eleuthera,
   Bahamas
   dreams and culture of, 1
   governor and Vice-Admiral of, 2
   recuperation on, 131, 133–34
   during WWII, 2–3
Bahamas General Hospital, 131, 133–34
bathing, sea-water, 62–63, 65
beer recollections, 60
biblical quotation books, 48, 58
bleaks, 2
Bligh, William, 9
blisters, skin, 100, 101
bodily functions, 55, 103

boils, skin, 87
Bounty (ship), 9

calendar, 49, *96*
cigarettes, 33, 48, 64
clothing, 48–49, 129–30
Columbus, Christopher, 4
compasses, 53, 94, 97
crabs, 112, 120
cramps, stomach, 70, 74, 86, 92, 93
Cruikshank, J. M., 132, 134

deaths
   Denny and Hawke, 82–84
   Morgan, 90
   Penny, 77–78
   Pilcher, 70–71
   Widdicombe, 135, 144
dehydration
   bodily functions, 55
   mouths and throats, condition of, 58,
      61, 62, 66–67, 93
   perspiration, 66
   salt water intake, 72–73
   sea-water bathing, 62–63, 65
   skin conditions, 61, 64, 87, 101, 102
delirium
   Morgan, 72–73, 74, 76, 77, 80, 85–86,
      87, 88–89

Pilcher, 67–68
Tapscott, 121
Denny, Barry Collingwood (Chief
      Mate—First Officer)
   death of, 82–84
   description, 30, 31
   escape in jolly-boat, 40–44
   illness, 70, 72, 74, 75, 76, 77
   jolly-boat destination plan, 45
   log book entries, 49–50, 51, 57, 60,
      63–64, 66, 68, 71
   night of attack, 52
   Pilcher's amputation plan, 68–69
destination plans, 45, 64
discipline, 73–74
dreams, 1–2, 7

Eleuthera, Bahamas
   description, 1–2, 3–4
   history of, 4–6
   rescue and recuperation on, 95, 109,
      126–33

fights, 73, 75, 76, 89, 123
fish, 108, 111–12, 124
fishing, 112
Flynn, Philip Robert Limpenny (Cap-
      tain), 29, 38
food cravings, 59–60, 66, 102, 105, 131
food supplies
   alternative, 120–21
   fish and shellfish, 108, 111, 112–13,
      120, 124
   rations, 57, 59, 68, 72
   seaweed, 73, 83, 87

gangrene, 58, 60, 65
Gerassimos, Michael, 130, 131
Gormley, Paddy, 28–29, 33, 34, 36
Governor's Harbor, Eleuthera, 6, 130

Harvard College, 5
Hawkes, Leslie (Third Engineer)
   command arguments, 75
   death of, 82–85
   description, 31
   escape in jolly-boat, 40–44

   log book entries by, 77, 79
   night of attack, 52
   water rationing arguments, 75–76
heat exposure, 61, 62–63, 65, 74, 87,
      100, 101
hound fish, 124
hurricanes, 115–19
Hyslop, William, 132

illnesses. See also dehydration
   delirium, 67–68, 72–73, 74, 76, 77,
      80, 85–86, 87, 88–89, 121
   melancholia, 134
   mood swings, 73, 76, 88, 89, 134
   nausea and vomiting, 70, 72, 74, 75,
      76, 77, 92
   stomach cramps, 70, 74, 86, 92, 93
   sunstroke and vertigo, 73, 86, 87, 88,
      121, 122
   wound infections, 58, 60, 65
insomnia, 134

Johnson, Lewis, 1–2, 6–8
Johnson, Mrs. Lewis, 1–2, 6–8, 129–30
jolly-boat
   calendar markings, 96
   description and equipment, 31,
      47–48
   discovery of, 7
   on Eleuthera Island, ii
   escape in, 37–44
   provisions, 9, 48, 50
   with Tapscott and Widdicombe, 110

Klein, Francis, 131

land sightings, 103, 121, 124–25
Leewards Islands, 45, 64
life-rafts, 31, 41–42
log books
   Denny's entries, 49–50, 51, 57, 60,
      63–64, 66, 68, 71
   Hawkes' entries, 77, 79
   Widdicombe's entries, 85, 90, 100,
      103, 104
lotteries, 64–65

melancholia, 134
mental clarity, 106, 122
mental deterioration
    delirium, 67–68, 72–73, 74, 76, 77,
        80, 85–86, 87, 88–89, 121
    melancholia, 134
    mood swings, 73, 76, 88, 89, 134
mirrors, 104
mood swings, 73, 76, 88, 89, 134
morale
    death and, 71, 78
    lotteries boosting, 64–65
    rations and, 60
    sleep and, 103
    suicide *vs.* will to live, 78, 82, 93, 94
Morgan, Leslie (second cook)
    attack experience, 51–52
    clothing, 49
    coma, 88, 89
    death of, 90
    description, 31
    mental deterioration, 72–73, 74,
        75–76, 77, 80, 85–86, 87, 88–89
    overboard rescue, 88
    sea water drinking, 87
    singing, 47
    will to live, 82
    wounds and condition, 46, 58,
        62, 66

Nassau, convalescence in, *13, 14, 95,
    109,* 132–34
nausea, 70, 72, 74, 75, 76, 77
navigation, 53, 64

Orford (ship), 23–24

pellagra, 131, 134
Penny, Richard (gunner)
    clothing, 49
    death of, 77–78
    description, 30
    escape in jolly-boat, 37
    night of attack, 36
    wounds and condition, 46, 65, 66,
        72, 75–76
perspiration, 66, 87, 100, 101

Pilcher, Roy Hamilton ("Second
    Sparks")
    clothing, 48
    death of, 70–71
    description, 30
    emergency provisions of, 47, 48
    escape in jolly-boat, 40–44
    lottery methodology, 65
    night of attack, 52
    rations refusal, 70
    wounds and condition, 43, 46, 50–51,
        58, 59, 60, 62, 65, 66, 67–69
Pittman, Cynthia, 20
prayers, 84
provisions
    of Bligh's *Bounty*, 9
    on jolly-boat, 9, 48, 50
    suggestions for, 74–75

rages, 2
rainstorms, 98–99, 102, 105, 113
rations. *See also* food supplies; water
        supplies
    life-boat stock suggestions, 74–75
    rationing amounts, 54–55, 57, 59, 68,
        72, 75–76, 77, 85
rescue and recuperation, 126–34
rudders, 81

salt water, drinking, 73, 83, 87
Sayle, William, 5
seaweed, 107, 111, 112
Segatoo, 4. *See also* Eleuthera, Bahamas
ship sightings, 55–56, 113–14
Siamese Prince (ship), 135, 144
singing, 47, 72–73
speed of travel, 65
starvation, 106–7, 134
storms, 2, 115–19
suicides, overboard, 77–79, 82–84, 90,
        92–94
sunstroke, 73, 86, 87, 88, 121, 122

Tapscott, Robert George "Bob"
    on *Anglo-Saxon*, 25–29
    background, 10–12, 15–17, 22–24
    on being at sea, 53

clothing, 49

convalescence in Nassau, *13*, *95*, *109*, 132–34

on Denny-Morgan overboard suicide, 83

escape in jolly-boat, 37, 39–44

food cravings, 59–60

foreboding of, 25, 32

illnesses, 86, 92, 121, 134

on jolly-boat with Widdicombe, *110*

morale, 76, 85

Morgan rescue, 88

night of attack, 34–37

notes to mother, 92–93

overboard suicide attempts, 92–93

Pilcher's amputation plan, 68–69

rescue and recuperation on Eleuthera, 7–8, 126–33

salt water intake, 73

Spark's mirror and, 104

temperment of, 28

water rationing, 76

Widdicombe relationship with, 28, 73, 101, 121–23

wounds, 46

urine, 92

vertigo, 73, 86, 122

vitamin deficiencies, 131, 134

water supplies

alternative, 92, 97

end of provisions, 85

rainstorms, 98–99, 102, 105, 113

rations, 54, 68, 75–76

salt water, 73, 83, 87

weather

heat and sun exposure, 61, 62–63, 65, 74, 87, 100, 101

hurricanes, 115–19

night temperatures, 77

rainstorms, 98–99, 102, 105, 113

wind, 58

weight loss, 62, 122

Weser (German raider ship), 34–42

whales, 108, 111

Widdicombe, Wilbert C. "Roy"

on *Anglo-Saxon*, 27–29

background, 17–21, 24–25

clothing, 49

as commander, 75, 85

convalescence in Nassau, *14*, *95*, *109*, 132–34

death of, 144

escape in jolly-boat, 39–44

food cravings, 59

on jolly-boat with Tapscott, *110*

log book entries by, 85, 90, 100, 103, 104

marriage of, 20, 24–25

mood swings, 73, 76, 88, 89

night of attack, 33–34, 37–39

overboard suicide attempts, 92–94

rescue and recuperation in Eleuthera, 7, 126–33

salt water intake, 73

stomach cramps, 92

sunstroke and vertigo, 73, 86, 87, 88, 121, 122

Tapscott relationship with, 28, 73, 101, 121–23

temperment of, 28, 29

will to live, 78, 82, 93

Windsor, Duchess of, *109*, 134–35

Windsor, Duke of, 2, *109*, 131, 134

World War II

bartering during, 21

declaration of war, 23

Eleuthera during, 2–3

shipping precautions during, 32

ships as soldier transports, 23–24

Spain during, 15–17

tourists during, 22

war zone seamen pay during, 15

Torpedo Sinks Furness Liner Siamese Prince

Seaman Who Survived 70 Days in Open Boat Last Fall Was One of Crew

The 8,456-ton Furness-Prince motor liner *Siamese Prince*, which left New York on February 3, was torpedoed and sunk on February 18th, off Scotland, it was learned here yesterday. Nothing was known here about the fate of her crew, among whom was Roy Widdicombe, twenty-one-year-old British sailor, who drifted 3,000 miles across the Atlantic last fall in an open boat with another seaman after a German raider had sunk their ship, the *Anglo-Saxon*, off the Azores.

Subsequent information from the steamship line was that "everyone on the *Siamese Prince* must be considered to be lost."